The Women of the Bible Speak

Also by Shannon Bream

Finding the Bright Side: The Art of Chasing What Matters

The
WOMEN
of the
BIBLE SPEAK

The WISDOM of 16 WOMEN
and THEIR LESSONS for TODAY

SHANNON BREAM

HarperCollins books may be purchased for educational, business, or sales promotional use. For information, please email the Special Markets Department at SPsales@harpercollins.com.

Fox News Books imprint and logo are trademarks of Fox News Network LLC.

FIRST EDITION

Illustrations by Erica Guillane-Nachez and ruskpp/stock.adobe.com

Library of Congress Control Number: 2021935852

ISBN 978-0-06-304659-7

22 23 24 25   LSC   30 29 28 27 26

To my grandmothers, Nell and Margaret,
whose stories rival those found in these pages:
Your deep faith has inspired me to believe God is present in
every valley and on every mountaintop. I love you most.

"She is clothed with strength and dignity; she can laugh at the days to come."

—Proverbs 31:25

CONTENTS

CONTENTS

"This time will be different. It has to be."

I often wonder what ran through the mind of the woman whose story is so powerful that it's woven through three of the Gospels—yet we don't even know her name. We do have plenty of details, though, about just how dire her situation was. She suffered with bleeding for twelve long years. During that time, she must have had moments of complete despondence.

In the time when she lived, this woman's affliction would have caused her not only physical pain, but also emotional isolation. According to custom, she would not have been able to worship in a temple, and many would have considered her unclean. This likely would have meant she couldn't touch the people she loved most: her own family and friends. She may have been banned from visiting markets or seeking any real community connections.

Mark tells us she "had suffered a great deal under the care of many doctors and had spent all she had, yet instead of getting better she grew worse" (Mark 5:26). After so many years, so many dead ends, there must have been times when she thought this was how her story would end: with her hopeless and helpless.

And yet, Mark goes on to tell us that "she had heard the reports about Jesus" (Mark 5:27). That was all it took for this disheartened woman to move forward.

Word of Jesus's miracles had spread far and wide, and crowds often followed Him, pushing in on every side, eager to hear His words and see if He could make a difference in their lives. The stories gave root to the tiniest seed of hope in the woman's heart, a little green shoot that gave her the courage to take a big risk. Matthew maps out her strategy: "[S]he said to herself, 'If I only touch his cloak, I will be healed'" (Matthew 9:21).

So, that was the entirety of her plan: to get as close to Jesus as possible, touch His cloak, and receive a miracle. Bold! Remember, she likely wasn't even supposed to leave her home, certainly not to be in a crowd where she would come in contact with other people—not to mention Jesus Himself. In her despair, she must have felt there were no other options left.

When she finally got to where Jesus was, He was on His way to attend to the request of a powerful man who had begged Him to save his dying daughter. As was often the case, this attracted spectators. Mark describes it as a "great crowd" that "thronged about him" (Mark 5:24). The ailing woman worked her way close enough to reach out to the miracle worker she'd heard so much about.

Luke shares the powerful moment in the simplest language, writing, "She came up behind him and touched the edge of his cloak, and immediately her bleeding stopped" (Luke 8:44).

Mark says, "Immediately her bleeding stopped and she felt in her body that she was freed from her suffering" (Mark 5:29). That was it! But the story still wasn't over.

Jesus knew what had happened. He looked to the crowd and asked His disciples who had touched Him. You can almost hear the laughter in Peter's voice as he replies, "Master, the people are crowding and pressing against you" (Luke 8:45). Here's the thing: the woman knew that a man so powerful that mere contact with

His garment would heal her would certainly figure out whom He had healed.

In both Mark and Luke, we're told that she went to Jesus in "fear and trembling," falling down before Him and telling Him "the whole truth." Was she afraid she was about to be exposed as an unclean rule-breaker who shouldn't even have been there? Jesus didn't berate or humiliate her in front of the enormous crowd hanging on His every word. Only He could have known in that moment just how much she had suffered or how she had courageously and humbly bundled all her hopes into the simple act of touching the hem of His garment. In all the Gospel accounts, He calls her "Daughter" and tells her, "Your faith has made you well." Think for a moment how those words must have felt to someone likely living as an outcast. Uttered, as they were, before the multitudes hanging on Jesus's every word, they would have constituted public acceptance.

Though *His power* was clearly the source of her healing, Jesus identified *her faith* as having activated her cure. After more than a decade of suffering, bad news, and financial ruin, she was finally free, healed in an instant—all because she dared reach out to Him for help when every earthly avenue had ended in nothing but loss and despair.

For many of us, 2020 was a year filled with pain: physical, financial, emotional, and mental. We often felt isolated, kept away from our loved ones, and disconnected from our houses of worship and the sense of community they provide. There were adversities we could not have imagined we'd face in our lifetimes. Hardships piled up, one on top of the other. And yet . . . there was hope. There was refuge. There was inspiration and healing.

Throughout the Bible, women are at the center of some of the most critical events. They were bold and brave, finding courage in the moments when everything hung in the balance. They were voices of truth and reason. They were steady and creative, following God's direction when it didn't make sense by the world's standards.

In this book, you'll hear their stories, watch the women come alive as we dig into their lives' significance. Individually, their accounts are powerful. Yet, here, we will consider the women in pairs, finding the commonalities in their callings and challenges. Some of the women knew one another. Others were connected simply by a thread of common purpose, one that becomes more illuminated as we study the women side by side. I pray you'll find comfort and hope as we take this journey together.

The Women of the Bible Speak

The Woman of the Little Spark

SARAH AND HAGAR

Women of the Covenants

SARAH
(Genesis 11:27–12:20; 16:1–6; 17:15–19; 18:1–15;
20:1–18; 21:1–13; 23:1–9)

The facts of Sarah's life sound like an adventure story, full of twists and turns: She was settled into her life when her husband suddenly announced they'd be upending everything they knew to move way out of their comfort zone. She managed a wealthy household with a very complicated blended family—and that's not all. She bore no child of her own, and even when God made her a specific promise, she laughed it off as impossible. How surprised she must have been when the wildly unthinkable finally came true for her—but oh, how far off track she'd already gotten by taking matters into her own hands.

According to the Bible, Abraham twice denied being Sarah's husband to protect himself when a powerful ruler noticed just how beautiful she was and wanted her for himself. In the case involving Pharaoh, Sarah was already sixty-five years old! Think about how enduringly stunning her beauty must have been to draw so much attention, even as she was entering her golden years.

While many details about Sarah are unknown, we do know this: she was definitely skeptical of men in shining robes telling ninety-year-old women they would have babies.

So, who was she, beyond these few tidbits? In reading the story of Abraham and Sarah, it's hard not to focus on Abraham. After all, he was the one who received the call from God: "Go from your country, your people and your father's household to the land I will show you" (Genesis 12:1). It's the first hint we receive that this land God will show him, the promised land, is going to play a crucial part in salvation history. But along with the promises to Abraham, God repeatedly makes clear that Sarah will be a key player, that she will be "a mother of nations; kings of peoples shall come from her" (Genesis 17:16).

If Sarah objected to their journey, Scripture does not record it. In order to avoid a famine, she and Abraham journeyed from Ur to Haran, from Haran to Canaan, and then from Canaan to Egypt. Sarah supported her husband during the dispute with his nephew Lot and during the subsequent battle with the five kings of Canaan, when he had to ride to Lot's rescue. In Egypt, she was beautiful enough to attract Pharaoh's notice, which prompted Abraham to fudge the truth about who she really was.

If you're wondering why Abraham felt compelled to lie, remember that he was a refugee traveling through a foreign land. This was a period when powerful rulers could claim beautiful women simply because they wanted them. A protesting husband could pay with his life, a consequence of which Abraham would have been all too aware.

Ultimately, the other men moved by Sarah's beauty rejected

her when they realized she was married. The Lord himself directly intervened to protect her by sending plagues, in the case of Pharaoh, and by visiting Abimelech with a warning. Abraham's fear put Sarah in danger and also put other men in a position where they could have sinned against God. Abraham's deceit didn't help anyone, and his behavior tells us something about his character: he was sometimes fearful and weak. In retrospect, it is rather remarkable that God chose a man like Abraham to be the patriarch of His chosen people, but perhaps He did this in order to demonstrate His power through Abraham's foolishness. As Paul notes in 2 Corinthians 12:9, God's "power is made perfect in weakness," and in 1 Corinthians 1:27, "God chose what is foolish in the world to shame the wise; God chose what is weak in the world to shame the strong."

In any case, Abraham's weakness of character had a marked influence on his marriage, and I often wonder how Sarah felt being placed in potential danger because of his decisions.

Sarah herself is voiceless until chapter 16 of the narrative, when, for the first time, she has something to say:

> Now [Sarah], [Abraham's] wife, had borne him no children. But she had an Egyptian slave named Hagar; so she said to [Abraham], "The Lord has kept me from having children. Go, sleep with my slave; perhaps I can build a family through her." [Abraham] agreed to what [Sarah] said. (Genesis 16:1–2)

It's almost as though Sarah were saying, *Okay, wait, hold up. I said nothing while you dragged us for hundreds of miles, from*

Chaldea to Canaan to Egypt and back again. I said nothing while you talked about this covenant with God that you somehow think you have and the special promises you say God has made you. But I've seen none of it happen, and if we're going to have an heir, then I'd better take matters into my own hands here.

The first time we hear Sarah speak, she has a plan, but we the readers know it's not God's plan. We know God is weaving an intricate story starring Isaac, but Sarah is still skeptical. Just the chapter before, God pledges to Abraham that "the one who will come from your own body shall be your heir" (Genesis 15:14). God had shown him the glittering night sky, promising him that his descendants would be as many as the stars in the sky: uncountable. Abraham was all in. The minute God said, *Jump*, Abraham said, *How high?* But highly uncertain that any of this would come to pass, Sarah wanted evidence. She appears to have been the practical one in the relationship. Not faithless, but not exactly trusting, either. So, she came up with the "solution" to what she saw as the problem of God's unfulfilled promise. Following ancient Near Eastern custom, Sarah hatched a plan to produce an heir: sending Abraham to "go into [her] maid," Hagar, so she could "obtain children through her."

But as sometimes happens when we stop trusting God's plan and go our own way, things went terribly wrong. The minute Hagar successfully conceived, the relationship between the two women imploded. In the Bible, Sarah complains to Abraham, "I put my slave in your arms, and now that she knows she is pregnant, she despises me" (Genesis 16:5). Hagar likely lorded her pregnancy over Sarah. Genesis 16:4 translates to show us that

Hagar considered Sarah a person of no standing because she was barren.

So, then, the far younger Hagar was the only one bearing a child for Abraham. It might have been natural for Hagar to assume that her relationship with both Sarah and Abraham had changed. Her status had surely improved, and as the mother of Abraham's sole heir, she had security for the future.

So, what was Abraham's reaction to the news that his wife's now-pregnant servant despised her? Did he urge calm? Did he try to hear both sides of the dispute? Not exactly. Abraham said to his wife, "Your slave is in your hands. Do with her whatever you think best" (Genesis 16:6).

This is now the second time we see Abraham acquiesce to his wife's wishes, when we know Sarah is in the wrong. Their relationship comes into sharper focus now, and it is a complicated one, marked by times when she speaks her mind and times when she silently follows his lead. In this instance, he attempted to restore peace in his relationship with Sarah by demolishing his relationship with the pregnant Hagar. *Do whatever you please,* he tells his wife, and Sarah does. The Bible tells us that Sarah "dealt harshly" with Hagar (Genesis 16:6). It's the same wording the Bible uses for the way the Egyptians treat their Jewish slaves in Exodus, meaning with oppression and forced labor. Abraham gave Sarah complete authority over Hagar, knowing what it would mean for the servant woman, and he stood by while Sarah abused the pregnant woman with impunity.

In reading any memoir or history of slavery in the American South or the Caribbean, we find the stories detailing the mistreatment of pregnant women the most gut-wrenching. It's impossible for us, as modern readers, to dredge up any sympathy for Sarah at this point. But like the men of the Bible, the women of the Bible are complicated. They are, on the whole, neither fully good nor completely bad people, but simply people, in all their messy and uncomfortable humanity. And it's when we can see them in their full humanity that God can teach us something about ourselves.

The next time we hear from Sarah, she is once again skeptical of God's plan. In one of the Bible's most enigmatic stories, God appears to Abraham at his tent by the oaks of Mamre and tells him that Sarah will bear a son. The story is a strange one because the first verse of the chapter says that "God appeared" to Abraham, but then the very next sentence says that "three men stood before him" (Genesis 18:1–2). Whatever happened at Mamre, it is clear that this was a very unusual visit. And this time, it wasn't just Abraham God had come to see.

"Where is your wife Sarah?" the three men ask him.

"There, in the tent," he says.

Then one of them says, "I will surely return to you about this time next year, and Sarah your wife will have a son" (Genesis 18:9,10).

This was a message for Sarah, loud and clear. When God appeared to Abraham before, He had told him that he would have a son of his body. This time, He was more explicit: it will be a son of Abraham's body *and* of Sarah's. She is central to this covenant narrative. She is an equal recipient of the promise, and it's almost as though God were saying, *Pay attention this time!*

Sarah did, and her reaction was immediate: she laughed! She laughed, one of the most extraordinary reactions to a revelation from God recorded in the Bible. However, don't forget, just one chapter earlier, Abraham was just as incredulous:

Abraham fell facedown; he laughed and said to himself, "Will a son be born to a man a hundred years old? Will Sarah bear a child at the age of ninety?" (Genesis 17:17)

At this point, Sarah was done with all revelations, all promises. She had seen enough. She had hoped long enough, she had tried long enough, she had twisted her life into knots enough. No more! And so, when the big reveal came, she laughed. *Tell me another*, Sarah thought.

And God took note.

"Why did Sarah laugh?" (Genesis 18:13), He asks. "Is anything impossible with God?" (Genesis 18:14). We can imagine Abraham turning several vivid shades of purple with embarrassment during this exchange. Sarah hastily tries to fix it, too. She denies laughing, but God responds, "No, you did laugh" (Genesis 18:15). The climactic moment of God's revelation to Abraham has just become the world's most disastrous dinner party.

We hear Sarah's voice in the text once more with the birth of Isaac, nine months later:

Now the Lord was gracious to Sarah as he had said, and the Lord did for Sarah what he had promised. Sarah became pregnant and bore a son to Abraham in his old age, at the very time God had promised him. Abraham gave the name Isaac to the son Sarah bore him. When his son Isaac was eight days old, Abraham circumcised him, as God commanded him. Abraham was a hundred years old when his son Isaac was born to him.

Sarah said, "God has brought me laughter, and everyone who hears about this will laugh with me." And she added, "Who would have said to Abraham that Sarah would nurse children? Yet I have borne him a son in his old age." (Genesis 21:1-7)

Sarah's laughter had been transformed: first into the name of the child and then into joy. Was she also laughing at her own disbelief and the renewal of her faith through this miraculous event? The laughter that at first she attempted to deny has now become an object of commemoration in the very name of her son, "Isaac"—or "Yitzchak" in the Hebrew, meaning "laughter." But that laughter is no longer the snide, mocking laughter of disbelief. It is now the laughter of joy, and Sarah invites others to join in it with her. It is the laughter of the reversal of all expectations, of resurrection, of hope reborn to new life. And her son's name is her nod of the head to God, her acknowledgment that not only was God right and she wrong, but that she, too, was included in the covenant and that she, too, was the recipient of promise.

It would be wonderful to end the story of Sarah here, but that is not where Scripture leaves her. For Sarah's story is intertwined with Hagar's from beginning to end, from Sarah's first words in the text, when she offers Hagar to Abraham, to her last words in the text, when she drives Hagar and Ishmael into the desert. Far from feeling calmer and more confident in God and in herself after Isaac's birth, Sarah seems instead to be on high alert.

When Isaac was three years old, the traditional age of weaning, Genesis 21 tells us that Sarah saw his older brother, Ishmael, "laughing"—some translations suggest "mocking." The Bible doesn't tell us anything more than that. Something about what she saw triggered a fresh backlash by Sarah. Did she feel that Ishmael's presence made her son seem less special, less extraordinary—after all, wasn't Ishmael a son of Abraham, too? And who was to say that, in later years, Ishmael might not grow jealous or full of hatred and threaten her beloved son? As we see again and again in the polygamous relationships the Bible documents, jealousy and division are almost always present among family members.

Sarah says to Abraham, "Get rid of that slave woman and her son, for that woman's son will never share in the inheritance with my son Isaac" (Genesis 21:10).

Did Sarah go too far this time in asking Abraham to end his relationship with his eldest son, to send him away so that he may never see him again? How could Sarah ask such a thing?

But nothing is a surprise to God or a barrier to His plans, and He reassured Abraham. God didn't tell Abraham that Sarah was right, but He did tell him that Ishmael would be a great nation, and under His protection. So, with that promise, perhaps Abraham felt confident that no harm would come to the boy or his mother and that, in order to preserve peace in his family, it would be best to send them away. So, off into the desert Hagar and Ishmael went, to a fate unknown to Sarah and Abraham.

We do not hear Sarah's voice again, though other voices in Scripture refer to her. She is called "the mother of promise" (Romans 9:9) and the "mother of faith" (Hebrews 11:11), and Peter refers to her as the model wife (1 Peter 3:6).

There is one more great event recorded in the life of Abraham and Sarah, before the narrative moves on to the next generation. God has a test in mind for Abraham: He asks him to take his one remaining child, the child of covenant and promise, his son

Isaac, and offer him as a human sacrifice. It is hard for us to imagine being asked to do the same with our own beloved children, but do not forget what Abraham had already witnessed: God's unending faithfulness. He had already watched as God kept His promise, bringing a newborn baby to a one-hundred-year-old man and his ninety-year-old wife. Hebrews 11:19 gives us insight into what Abraham must have been thinking:

> By faith Abraham, when God tested him, offered Isaac as a sacrifice. He who had embraced the promises was about to sacrifice his one and only son, even though God had said to him, "It is through Isaac that your offspring will be reckoned." Abraham reasoned that God could even raise the dead, and so in a manner of speaking he did receive Isaac back from death.

Because Abraham had already heard God's promises and seen them come to fruition, Hebrews is suggesting that Abraham believed that, even if he were called to sacrifice Isaac, God could bring him back to life.

Did Abraham tell Sarah what he was doing? This is the great question. He didn't tell Isaac, which is understandable. Not only did he need the child's compliance, but he didn't want to frighten him.

The story of Abraham trudging toward the spot where God had called him to sacrifice Isaac is a difficult one to read. We now know the end of the story, but in those hours and days, Abraham couldn't have known how things would unfold. Genesis 22:6 reveals his deep faith in the journey:

He said to his servants, "Stay here with the donkey while I and the boy go over there. We will worship and then we will come back to you."

He is stating his clear belief that the two will return together, despite what God is asking of him.

Isaac must have been bewildered, even frightened at some point, as Abraham followed through, reaching for the very knife "to slay his son . . .":

. . . the angel of the Lord called out to him from heaven, "Abraham! Abraham!"
"Here I am," he replied.
"Do not lay a hand on the boy," he said. "Do not do anything to him. Now I know that you fear God, because you have not withheld from me your son, your only son." (Genesis 22:10)

And then, of course, the bleating of the ram in the thicket, quickly retrieved to become the sacrifice instead of Isaac. The high drama of it makes for an incomparable story, but Sarah saw none of it. All this happened out of her sight and, perhaps, her knowledge.

If God had applied the same test to Sarah, what would she have done? From what we know of Sarah, it's hard to believe she would have saddled that donkey and taken her son to be sacrificed. It's hard to imagine any mother who has borne a child in her body saying yes to that. How does any of us react when our faith is put to the test, whether through periods of doubt and despair, the death of a loved one, infertility, or financial ruin? Often, we are asked to be *willing* to sacrifice what feels most precious to us. Do we, as Abraham did, proceed in faith or look for our own way out? Sarah, who longed so desperately for her own child, made a decision that forever altered history. And yet God chose her to be the human fulfillment of His covenant with Abraham, "the mother of Israel the nation" (Isaiah 51:2). Again, despite our flaws, we can be used by our Heavenly Father to weave together His highest purposes. Sarah is the perfect illustration of that beautiful, complex truth.

ℋAGAR
(Genesis 16:1–16, 21:8–21)

Of all the women we are looking at in the pages of this book, Hagar is the only non-free person. Many Bible translations define her status as "maidservant," which makes her sound like someone who showed up to do semi-regular cleaning. While the language in Genesis 16 suggests she is a trusted servant of Sarah's, by Genesis 21, the language shifts to indicate that Hagar is by then viewed as no more than a slave. She was not free to come and go as she pleased, but was the property of her owner, Sarah. This is the dominant feature of Hagar's life and the one that colors everything else we know about her and her situation.

The Bible tells us that Hagar is an Egyptian. It makes sense that Sarah might have acquired her when she and Abraham lived in Egypt during the time of famine described in Genesis 12:10, when she and Abraham practiced their deception on Pharaoh by telling him that she was Abraham's sister, not his wife. It's possible Abraham and Sarah were figures of some wealth and power by the time of their sojourn in Egypt. After all, most people traveling to Egypt probably weren't worried about what they would tell Pharaoh, as common people didn't usually come in contact with royalty. However, Genesis 12:15 tells us it is Sarah's great presence that attracts the high-level attention. A person with disposable wealth might well have acquired slaves in Egypt, which he would then have transported with him back to Canaan. And Hagar did not appear to be just any slave, hired to tend to the camels and cook; she was the personal attendant of Abraham's wife, Sarah.

The facts we know of Hagar's life are few and simple. She was offered to Abraham as a concubine by Sarah. (As a servant, Hagar would not have been asked her opinion on the matter.) She bore Abraham's firstborn son, Ishmael, and was then entangled in a combative relationship with Sarah, compelled to leave not once but twice—first, while pregnant and, again, later (for good), after Sarah's son was born. These short, brutal facts make it hard not to feel compassion for her.

But Hagar's life (and its impact) is so much larger than what happens to her in the pages of Genesis. Her story goes on. Paul himself, in Galatians, shows how her life illustrates important lessons for Christians:

> For it is written that Abraham had two sons, one by the slave woman and the other by the free woman. His son by the slave woman was born according to the flesh, but his son by the free woman was born as the result of a divine promise.

> These things are to be taken figuratively: the women represent two covenants. One covenant is from Mount Sinai and bears children who are to be slaves. This is Hagar.

> Now you, brothers and sisters, like Isaac, are children of promise.
> Therefore, brothers and sisters, we are not children of the slave woman, but of the free woman. (Galatians 4:22-24, 28, 31)

Paul draws a simple but powerful equation: Hagar and her son represent a condition of bondage, and Sarah and her son represent freedom. For Paul, Christianity means freedom, and observing the Jewish law means bondage. The law was good, but it had no power to free the human race from the slavery of sin. It was the covenant promise, which flowed through Sarah and Isaac, that brought freedom through Christ. Here, Paul is talking to Gentile Christians who have converted to Christ but who question whether they must also observe Jewish law. *What are you doing?* Paul says. *You already have everything you need for salvation, and you don't need to be adding more burdens to yourself!* Paul rebukes some who infiltrated the Church in Galatia, arguing that members need not only trust in Christ but also keep all the old Jewish laws and traditions. He nudges new believers to look deeper than the literal meaning of the text, to discover the spiritual truths inside it. And in the process of doing that, Hagar becomes a symbol.

For Christians who were deeply in love with Jesus and seeing Him everywhere, this kind of symbolic reading became a natural way to see Christ in the pages of the Bible. In 1 Corinthians, Paul talks about the miraculous rock from which the Hebrew people drank when in the wilderness: "All ate the same spiritual food," he says, "and all drank the same spiritual drink. For they drank of that spiritual Rock which followed them, and that Rock was Christ" (1 Corinthians 10:3-4). For these early Christians, Christ and His truth appeared symbolically everywhere in the Scriptures. Suddenly, the pages of the Bible were illuminated! Christians continued to read the Scriptures this way through the generations, and especially the Hagar story. In later Christian writings, Hagar came to mean bondage not just to the law, but to the entire sinful condition of humanity—the city of this world. The unredeemed were the "children of Hagar," exiles from the body of Christ and from heaven itself.

In all these symbolic readings, it is easy to lose sight of Hagar the person—because before she was anything else, Hagar was a person, a vulnerable woman without any real protectors in the world, an enslaved woman who was never given any choices, a mother who wanted life and happiness for her son. If we can separate Hagar from the layers of symbolism heaped on her by later generations, we can recover some sense of who she was and what she might have to say to us today.

We meet Hagar in two incidents, and they both involve her mistress, Sarah. God had promised children to Abraham, but Sarah had given him none. That's when Sarah hatched her plan to offer Hagar as Abraham's concubine, in the hope of providing him with a legal heir. After Hagar became pregnant, her relationship with Sarah changed. We learn that when Hagar learned she was pregnant, "she began to despise her mistress" (Genesis 16:4). The Hebrew here is as enigmatic as the English, but it appears Hagar holds Sarah in lower regard because, while she herself is fertile, her mistress remains barren.

Hagar's change of attitude is understandable. After all, the likelihood is that she wasn't consulted about becoming a concubine in the first place, just as she wasn't consulted about being purchased by Sarah and Abraham. Her life and her body were not her own. Being pregnant with the master's child was her first opportunity for a kind of freedom. Suddenly, she was not just disposable property. She had worth! But that worth was not because of who she was, but because of the child inside her. It must have been bittersweet to realize that, finally, she would be a person of value, but that that value would be attached to her child, not to her. Still, any value was better than no value. Hagar might well have assumed that from then on, things would be different. She might have assumed that the sort of menial labor she was doing before would no longer be required of the woman bearing the master's child. And Sarah—who so conspicuously could not bear the master's child—might have resented her for it, no matter what Hagar did.

Again and again, the Bible presents us with the struggle over infertility. We will see this drama play itself out again in Rachel and Leah, and in Hannah. For women of the Bible, fertility meant more than just the love of a child. It meant more than just a way for a woman to gain security and status in the world. Fertility was often viewed as divine favor itself. Some believed that to bear a child was to wear a mark of God's love, and to be barren was therefore a mark of God's displeasure. But it's important to note that from the moment God creates Eve, she is a person of value because she is created in His very image. In our Heavenly Father's eyes, we as women are treasured and honored wholly and apart from the gift of motherhood. (Much more on Rachel, Leah, and Hannah in the chapters ahead.)

Did Hagar show Sarah compassion as she suffered this agony and humiliation? We see no indication that there was any tenderness in their relationship, or any mutual caring. Whatever bond they did have was probably ruptured by Hagar's pregnancy. Sarah mistreated the pregnant Hagar, and Hagar did the sensible thing: she ran away. It wasn't just herself she had to look after, but also her unborn child. And Abraham made it clear that he was unwilling to protect her, even if she was pregnant with his child. So, Hagar ran to the wilderness, probably hoping to find some solution there, or another path in life, or some kind of escape. What she found instead was the angel of the Lord:

> The angel of the Lord found Hagar near a spring in the desert; it was the spring that is beside the road to Shur. And he said, "Hagar, slave of Sarai, where have you come from, and where are you going?"
> "I'm running away from my mistress Sarai," she answered.
> Then the angel of the Lord told her, "Go back to your mistress and submit to her." (Genesis 16:7–9)

The first thing to note here is that if the "angel of the Lord" asks you where you're going, it's a sure bet He already knows. But God always gives us an opportunity to be honest with him. Think about the first question God asks in the Bible: "Adam, where are you?" In much the same way, the angel here asked Hagar, inviting her to be honest—which she was. But God's answer was not an easy one. God told her to go back, to give up her hard-won freedom. How much Hagar must have wanted to shout, "No!" The thought of going back must have been unbearable. And then came the difficult words that none of us ever wants to hear: humble yourself. What a seemingly impossible, painful thing God was asking of her.

This is the first appearance of the angel of the Lord in the Bible. And this mighty angel doesn't come to a king or to a priest, but to a pregnant slave girl who is alone and cowering in fear in the wilderness. She had no defender or encourager in this world, and yet the God of heaven wanted Hagar to know that He saw and heard her in her distress.

The angel tells her that "the Lord has heard of your misery" (Genesis 16:11). This must have been astonishing news, for more than one reason. For one thing, Hagar was not of Abraham's family. She was Egyptian, not even from Abraham's home of

Ur. She probably didn't even speak their language all that well, and there's a good chance she did not worship the strange and singular God they worshipped. Why would that God care about her? But He came to her, in her fear and her desolation. He *saw* her.

So, who was it Hagar saw, exactly? After the angel of the Lord told her to go back to Sarah, he delivered a promise. He gave her a message, using words that (for a Christian) echo the words spoken by another, much later, angel:

> **"You are now pregnant and you will give birth to a son. You shall name him Ishmael . . ." (Genesis 16:11)**

But when the visitation was done, what did Hagar say? As far as she was concerned, she had a direct and unmediated vision of God Himself. She even gave God a name—the first person in the Bible to do so:

> **She gave this name to the Lord who spoke to her: "You are the God who sees me," for she said, "I have now seen the One who sees me." (Genesis 16:13)**

She said that the one who appeared to her was "El Ro-i," which means, literally, "the God of seeing." God had seen her, and she had seen God. Hagar had been perfectly seen and known. Think about what that must have meant for an enslaved woman. How many eyes had looked right past or through her in her life? Visitors to Abraham's tent, people in the slave market of Egypt—she would have been no more than furniture to them, something people glanced at and then away from. She was used to being unseen. But this God was not like that. God looked right at her, and for the first time in her life, Hagar was seen.

An experience like that might have made it possible for her to go back to Sarah. Once you have looked into the eyes of God and seen Him looking back at you, even the impossible can seem doable. In the passage just before this one, God appears to Abraham and seals His covenant with him. The Bible tells us that God came to him "in a vision," and that Abraham heard "the voice of the Lord" (Genesis 15:1). Their covenant was sealed. But in Hagar's case, God appeared and offered His love and compassion. He gave her what she likely wanted and needed most: someone to see her as she truly was.

The knowledge of that God stayed with Hagar in her second trial, too, a time when the power of His words must have served as some comfort when things went from bad to worse. After Sarah was finally granted her child, and Isaac was three years old, Hagar was sent away in a more formal sense, the Bible's language suggesting a deliberate action that may have stripped away Hagar's identity, her inheritance, and likely her hope. It did her no good that she was the mother of Abraham's firstborn son; once again, the father of her child failed to defend her. Abraham had God's assurance that Hagar and Ishmael would be fine, but the Bible doesn't tell us if he shared that assurance with Hagar. She was sent off into the punishing desert with the bare minimum of supplies, and it wasn't enough to sustain the two of them. Hagar was quickly out of options:

When the water in the skin was gone, she put the boy under one of the bushes. Then she went off and sat down about a bowshot away, for she thought, "I cannot watch the boy die." And as she sat there, she began to sob. (Genesis 21:15-16)

In one of the most heartrending passages in Scripture, Hagar acknowledges that watching her son's death will be the final grief she cannot bear. She despaired. Everyone had abandoned her, and she could no longer keep her son safe from a world that had no use for a slave woman's son.

Many of us are fortunate enough to live in a world where we don't have to fear every day for our children's lives or safety. We tell ourselves that we have made them safe, that the trappings of middle-class life can keep them safe. If we are privileged enough, we enroll them in good schools, take them to good doctors, keep a close eye on their activities. All too often, though, we fail to consider the anguish of mothers who can't do these things for their children. For the poor and downtrodden in this world, these basic safeguards are often unattainable. For those mothers whose children face hatred and discrimination, safety is often impossible to guarantee. And the truth is, all of us are all one terrible, unimaginable catastrophe away from being in Hagar's shoes.

But God was not done with Hagar:

God heard the boy crying, and the angel of God called to Hagar from heaven and said to her, "What is the matter, Hagar? Do not be afraid; God has heard the boy crying as he lies there. Lift the boy up and take him by the hand, for I will make him into a great nation." (Genesis 21:17-18)

God reached into Hagar's despair and sent an angel to speak gentle and comforting words to her. The angel said to her the words that angels say again and again in the Bible: *Do not fear!* These words are said by an angel for the first time in the Bible when they are said to Hagar—the same words an angel says to Zechariah and to Mary, to Joshua and to the women at Jesus's tomb. They are also the words God Himself speaks to Abraham when He says, "Do not be afraid! I am your shield and will be your exceedingly great reward" (Genesis 15:1). Hagar is addressed in the same words that God uses for Abraham because this is the God who truly sees and who recognizes no distinction between the wealthy patriarch and the sorrowful slave. The "God Who Sees" is the God who sees not with the eyes of the world, but with the eyes of heaven.

How might Hagar's and Sarah's stories have been different if their relationship had been different? If they had found a way to connect with each other, to forgive each other, to understand each other's grief, what would have changed? What would have been the same? It could be that all that would have been necessary was for Hagar to have reached out to her mistress with compassion and generosity, even if Sarah showed her none. Kindness to someone who has been unkind to us is hard, but what about kindness to someone who has been unjust to us for years and years? Or kindness to someone who has oppressed us? That's where the hard starts to seem impossible.

But if Hagar had found a way to extend that hand, then Sarah might not have driven her away. Alternatively, if Sarah had been willing to overlook Hagar's disrespect and recognize how insecure she felt, perhaps she could have found commonalities between them. Both women were valued by God, who cherished and understood them. What if they had reflected their covenant with God by entering into a covenant with each other? It's possible that in a world like that, Ishmael and Isaac could have grown up together. What would it have looked like, a world in which the ancestor of the Jews and the ancestor of the Arabs had grown up arm in arm, as beloved brothers who could not bear to be separated? It isn't just human hearts that might have been different then, but the map of the world. Who knows what future maps our hearts can rewrite if we can somehow find our way to compassion for one another?

Sarah and Hagar Study Questions
---

1. God appears to Abraham six times. Take a look at each of those six times and figure out what God is asking of him in each of these appearances.

   > Genesis 12:1–3 (the instruction to leave Haran)
   >
   > Genesis 15:1–21 (the first covenant)
   >
   > Genesis 17:1–22 (the renewed covenant)
   >
   > Genesis 18:1 (the appearance at the oaks of Mamre)
   >
   > Genesis 18:20 (Abraham pleads for Sodom)
   >
   > Genesis 22:1–18 (Moriah)

2. What is the relationship of Sarah to each of these appearances? In which ones is she involved? In which ones is she absent? Which ones seem to apply to her, and which ones don't? When we read the Bible, it's important to look beyond just the passage we're reading. The Bible's divisions into chapters happened only in the medieval era, almost a thousand years after some of these texts were written. So, for ancient readers, there was no real break between what came before a passage and what came after it. How might that change what we see of Sarah in these six passages?

   For instance, look at the covenant passage of Genesis 15:1–21. If we are reading like an ancient reader, we see that this passage goes immediately into Sarah's discussion with Abraham about Hagar and having an heir through her maidservant. What does this tell us about

Sarah's relationship to the covenant? What does it tell us about her relationship to Abraham? What does it tell us about her relationship to God?

3. The Bible tells us that Sarah died and was buried in the field Abraham had bought—his first foothold in the land of Canaan, the purchase that turned him from a nomad into a landowner, a stakeholder in the community of Canaan. What is the very first action that Abraham undertakes after her death? Take a look at Genesis 24:1–8. What does this tell us about the importance of Sarah to Abraham? What does it tell us about the importance of Sarah to Isaac?

4. Hagar leaves Abraham and Sarah twice. The first time (Genesis 16:6–14), God sends her back. The second time (Genesis 21:14–21), Abraham and Sarah send her away. What is the difference between the two times? Has anything changed in Hagar between these two events?

RACHEL AND LEAH

Sisters and Rivals

RACHEL
(Genesis 29:1–30:24, 31:31–35, 35:16–20)

The story of Jacob and Rachel is a fascinating account of love, deception, and jealousy—and is more outlandish than just about any reality show today. Here, for the first time in the Bible, we see a romantic attachment that looks a lot like what we are used to—maybe even that fairytale concept of "love at first sight." All the pairs of husbands and wives we see before this—Adam and Eve, Abraham and Sarah, Isaac and Rebekah—are the result of some outside intervention. These marriages probably resulted in love between the spouses, but the fact remains that the pairs didn't come together in the way most couples do today. That just wasn't how families worked in that time and place. Marriages were transactional in nature: often just as much an alliance of family and property as of two people. And then came Jacob and Rachel.

The story of Rachel is inseparable from the story of her husband, Jacob; she was the end and object of his quest. When we first meet Jacob, we find that he's in a rivalry with his twin brother, Esau. Jacob was his mother's favorite, while Esau held his father's affection. It was over a bowl of stew that Jacob first cheated his brother out his inheritance. And then, as their father lay on his death bed, Jacob pulled off a scam that also stripped Esau of his blessing as firstborn. Finally, Esau had had enough.

Esau intended to kill Jacob as soon as their father, Isaac, died. Their mother warned Jacob and counseled him to flee to her brother Laban's home, far away. It was on the way there that Jacob had his famous vision of the stairway, or ladder, between earth and heaven, with the angels ascending and descending it.

> There above it stood the Lord, and he said: "I am the Lord, the God of your father Abraham and the God of Isaac. I will give you and your descendants the land on which you are lying. Your descendants will be like the dust of the earth, and you will spread out to the west and to the east, to the north and to the south. All peoples on earth will be blessed through you and your offspring. I am with you and will watch over you wherever you go, and I will bring you back to this land. I will not leave you until I have done what I have promised you." (Genesis 28:13–15)

Jacob the scam artist, who was out to get out of life what he could, no matter whom he had to trample, was suddenly shown a vision of a life much larger than his own. He was given a blessing and a promise by God Himself, and it changed his life. The God of Abraham and Isaac had reached down to Jacob—a God in whom, we can imagine, Jacob hadn't been too interested up to this point.

Immediately after this vision at Bethel, Jacob encountered Rachel. Moses, the writer of Genesis, intentionally placed their meeting immediately after the vision. Was Jacob seeing the world with fresh eyes after that divine encounter? He was clearly overcome with emotion when he met Rachel by the well, and he realized that of all the people he could have encountered as he fled from the threat of death, she would take him one step closer to safety.

> When Jacob saw Rachel[,] daughter of his uncle Laban, and Laban's sheep, he went over and rolled the stone away from the mouth of the well and watered his uncle's sheep. Then Jacob kissed Rachel and began to weep aloud. He had told Rachel that he was a relative of her father and a son of Rebekah. So she ran and told her father. (Genesis 29:10–12)

After Jacob worked for Laban for a month, Laban asked the younger man what wages he could pay him. Jacob, smitten, asked for the one thing he desired most:

> Jacob was in love with Rachel and said, "I'll work for you seven years in return for your younger daughter Rachel." Laban said, "It's better that I give her to you than to some other man. Stay here with me." So Jacob served seven years to get Rachel, but they seemed like only a few days to him because of his love for her. (Genesis 29:18–20)

Can you imagine making this deal with your future father-in-law? Seven years! And the Bible tells us it seemed like only a few days because of how much he loved her.

But here is where we see the ultimate double-crosser get exactly what he dished out to his brother, and the betrayal comes from his uncle, Laban. You see, Rachel and Jacob weren't alone in this fairy tale. Rachel had an older sister, Leah, and here's how the Bible describes them:

> Leah had weak eyes, but Rachel had a lovely figure and was beautiful. (Genesis 29:17)

Rachel probably had all the prospects in the world, but Laban wanted to get his older daughter married first, so he laid a trap for Jacob at the altar. After a night of feasting, Laban substituted Leah for Rachel, and Jacob didn't figure this out until the next morning.

> So Jacob said to Laban, "What is this you have done to me? I served you for Rachel, didn't I? Why have you deceived me?" (Genesis 29:25)

Jacob was outraged, but it didn't dim his love for Rachel, and he certainly doesn't appear to blame her: "[H]is love for Rachel was greater than his love for Leah," the Scripture tells us (Genesis 29:30). We also see he made a deal with Laban.

> "Finish this daughter's bridal week; then we will give you the younger one also, in return for another seven years of work." (Genesis 29:27)

And that's exactly what Jacob did. Fourteen years of labor to finally settle the debt for the woman he fell for the first time he saw her shepherding her father's flock in the fields.

How must all this have felt to Rachel, watching as Leah was married to Jacob and not her and knowing she was the object of his undying affection? Had she been counting on the plan: that she would marry a handsome man who had fallen deeply in love with her? Watching her sister go off to bed with Jacob on what should have been her own honeymoon turned her fairy tale into a nightmare. Even worse, it was a gut-wrenching betrayal involving her sister. What happened to her relationship with Leah? We don't know much about their relationship before Jacob arrived on the scene, but it seems it went steadily downhill after that.

Rachel's frustrations only mounted when her sister was able to conceive when she could not. But imagine how Leah must have felt during this time? God had mercy on her.

When the Lord saw that Leah was not loved, he enabled her to conceive, but Rachel remained childless. (Genesis 29:31)

More on Leah to come.

When Rachel saw that she was not bearing Jacob any children, she became jealous of her sister. So she said to Jacob, "Give me children, or I'll die!" Jacob became angry with her and said, "Am I in the place of God, who has kept you from having children?" (Genesis 30:1–2)

Not only does Scripture give us a dramatic love story in Jacob and Rachel, but it also reminds us that conflict in marriage has been around for ages. Rachel took to her husband what she thought was a legitimate grievance, and he reminded her that it was God who was in charge of her destiny. For Rachel, this was deeply personal. As we saw in the story of Sarah, fertility in the ancient world was about much more than just having children. Fertility, the life created and carried by women, was considered a sign of God's favor. For Rachel, her lack of fertility must have felt like a curse. Was infertility to be her reward for everything she had gone through? She had waited seven long years for her chance to marry Jacob and have children. Surely, God would reward her! But it seemed she got only heartache instead.

One of the stages of grief, counselors tell us, is bargaining. We say to God, *Okay, what do I have to do to undo this pain and get what I want?* Seen this way, Rachel's life appears to be one long stage of grief, because she is constantly bargaining. She is always looking for a way to "fix" her situation, and in that she is very much like the man she married.

Rachel's first attempt at "solving" her problem was the same strategy we saw Sarah deploy. When Sarah doubted that God's promise to her would ever come to fruition, she took matters into her own hands. Rachel proposed the same deal that Sarah had given Abraham: have a child with my servant. Rachel offered her servant Bilhah to Jacob in her place, intending to then raise Bilhah's children as her own—and this seemed to work.

> Then Rachel said, "God has vindicated me; he has listened to my plea and given me a son." Because of this she named him "Dan." Rachel's servant Bilhah conceived again and

bore Jacob a second son. Then Rachel said, "I have had a great struggle with my sister, and I have won." So she named him Naphtali. (Genesis 30:6–8)

The names Rachel gave these little boys tell us more about her than they do about who the boys will become. Rachel watched as Leah gave Jacob son after son, and she viewed their situation as the ultimate in sibling rivalry. Whatever love and compassion or sisterly closeness ever existed, it was now long gone. There is a parallel here between Rachel's struggles with her sister and Jacob's divine wrestling match just ahead in Genesis 32. Rachel knew God had closed her womb, so her battles were twofold. She was grappling with both God and "man"—her own sister in particular.

Rachel's story exposes such a human vulnerability. What happened in her life so often happens in ours as well. All of us will experience grief, a loss, or a situation beyond our control. What do we do when those moments come? All too often, it's easy to look for someone to blame. *This wouldn't have happened if I hadn't done this, or if I hadn't said that, or if I hadn't made a mistake*, we say to ourselves. From the Garden of Eden, when Adam shifts the blame to "the woman You gave me" (Genesis 3:12), all the way to Rachel, Genesis is filled with stories of people playing the blame game.

We blame other people not just because it relieves us of responsibility, but because it can be comforting to think that there are outside reasons for our pain, some kind of purpose in it. Rachel wanted to blame Jacob or her sister or God Himself, but when we are in the midst of our darkest valleys, it's often impossible for our human minds to find an explanation, or at least one that makes sense. Recall that even Jesus's disciples were puzzled by the idea that bad things could happen without anyone being at fault. "Rabbi, who sinned," they ask Him when they see a man who is blind from birth, "this man or his parents?" (John 9:2). Jesus answers them:

> "Neither this man nor his parents sinned," said Jesus, "but this happened so that the works of God might be displayed in him." (John 9:3)

Tragedy in the human realm isn't always the result of God's judgment, but it does always present an opportunity to show His glory.

It's likely Rachel couldn't see that far ahead, feeling only that she was being judged by God and that her sentence of infertility was connected to God's favoring her sister. Rachel viewed it as a battle, and she wanted victory. Hadn't Jacob himself engaged in some pretty sketchy behavior in order to get the upper hand over his brother? Rachel's life became laser-focused on this contest with her sister, and she was willing to do whatever it took to win.

For its next installment of the "Rachel versus Leah" story, the Bible includes a very curious episode involving a mandrake plant. For centuries, many people believed the mandrake's roots could cure infertility, aid conception, and promote love. So, when Leah's eldest son, Reuben, found some mandrake plants, the desperate Rachel wanted one. She swallowed her pride and approached her sister with this startling proposition.

> Rachel said to Leah, "Please give me some of your son's mandrakes." But she said to her, "Wasn't it enough that

you took away my husband? Will you take my son's mandrakes too?" "Very well," Rachel said, "he can sleep with
you tonight in return for your son's mandrakes." (Genesis
30:14–15)

It's hard to read this passage and not think, *Does Jacob have a
say in all this?* The two sisters' personalities and struggles over
winning his affection and bearing him children left Jacob looking like a rag doll dragged back and forth between two quar-
reling women. Rachel was willing to trade away time with her
husband in return for access to that mandrake root. Rachel already had Jacob's attention, but she had also become obsessed
with getting the upper hand on her sister by bearing him children as well. Did Jacob ever look at his wife and think about his
own burning desire to one-up Esau? Did he want to say to her,
Stop! I know where this ends?

Finally, Rachel got what she was after. It was not because of the
mandrake root or because of the willing Bilhah. It was because
of her own fervent prayers:

Then God remembered Rachel; he listened to her and enabled her to conceive. She became pregnant and gave
birth to a son and said, "God has taken away my disgrace."
She named him Joseph, and said, "May the Lord add to me
another son." (Genesis 30:22–24)

In the end, Scripture tells us that "God listened to her." It
wasn't any of her plans and schemes that bore fruit, but her
heartfelt prayer to God. We cannot bargain with our Heavenly
Father, but we can know that He hears our prayers and knows

the deepest desires of our hearts. In the midst of our most profound pain, there is often great relief in laying all our hurts and fears before our Heavenly Father. He already knows the turmoil or trials in our lives, but there's something freeing about talking to Him, unloading our burdens and taking up His assurances to serve as our strength and our shield, our refuge and hiding place.

This is a truth that the Psalms illustrate well. They aren't sanitized. They're filled with worries about life-and-death threats, people lying in wait and in deep grief over sin and loss. The Psalms teach us that God does not want our whitewashed selves, but our actual selves—even the parts of us that want to get even, that harbor hatred, that cry out in agony and frustration to God. Prayer can be a place of utter honesty, and no lasting growth can happen in our spiritual lives until we can get to that place. There, we can receive God's answers. Sometimes they point to a different, better path than we expected. Other times, they align with our desires. For Rachel, the answer was her son, a son who would go on to save the rest of his brothers and his entire family.

But the story of Rachel and Leah does not end with their discord. We read no more about the struggle between the sisters. The next time we see them, they are united, and Jacob has seen the writing on the wall and knows it is time to leave Laban's territory. He also knows that Laban is not likely to let him go quietly, not after all the wealth he has acquired while working for his father-in-law.

So, Jacob approached Laban, asking to leave with his family after many years of work. Laban begged Jacob to stay and made him a deal, mapping out exactly which livestock Jacob could take as his own. But the deal went south:

> Then the Lord said to Jacob, "Go back to the land of your fathers and to your relatives, and I will be with you." (Genesis 31:3)

Jacob told Rachel and Leah that he perceived a negative change in the way Laban now viewed him. He then went on to rehearse for them, in detail, how it was that God had led him to acquire much wealth and how it was under God's hand that he had prospered. He told them about Bethel and his experiences with God there. He laid the groundwork for why he was planning to leave Laban and the land of their birth.

If we don't pay careful attention, we can miss why this is such a remarkable passage. There is no other passage in the Old Testament in which a man speaks at such length and with such detail to a woman, much less a pair of women. But Jacob wants to include Rachel and Leah in the reasoning behind his decision. Then, for the first and only time, the sisters speak as one: Rachel and Leah say to him, "Do we still have any share in the inheritance of our father's estate?" (Genesis 31:14). The sisters found their unity at last, as often happens when we face an outside threat. Jacob might have wondered if, when it came down to it, his wives felt they were more Laban's daughters than his, Jacob's, wives. Any doubt he had was put to rest by their resounding vote of confidence in him and by their rejection of their father.

In no time, Jacob was back to the scheming of his early days, hatching a plan to disappear suddenly. It wasn't exactly a complex, carefully thought-out plot.

> Moreover, Jacob deceived Laban the Aramean by not telling him he was running away. So he fled with all he had, crossed the Euphrates River, and headed for the hill country of Gilead. (Genesis 31:20)

Once Laban discovered the hasty escape, he spent seven days chasing after Jacob, until he found him and the daughters who had left him behind. There was clearly tension between the two men, and heated words over why Laban hadn't even been permitted to kiss his daughters and grandchildren good-bye. But Laban had heard from the Lord and knew he wasn't to harm Jacob, so the men agreed to a covenant between them, a keeping of the peace.

> Early the next morning Laban kissed his grandchildren and his daughters and blessed them. Then he left and returned home. (Genesis 30:55)

The next time we see Rachel should be a joyful one for her. Once again, she has been blessed with a son, but the story does not have a happy ending. As many women in her day did, she struggled and died in childbirth. As she was dying, she named her son "Ben-Oni," meaning "son of my misfortune." But Jacob undid her dying wish, not out of disrespect, but as a way to honor his beloved wife. He renamed his last son "Benjamin," meaning "son of my good fortune." It was Rachel who was his right hand for so many years. The pillar he erected on her grave recalls the pillar he established in Bethel, at the place of his vision. In that place, God had promised him:

> "Your descendants will be like the dust of the earth, and you will spread out to the west and to the east, to the north and to the south." (Genesis 28:14)

Rachel was a key player in that heavenly promise God made to Jacob. Children were the deepest desire of her heart, but it seems she never stopped being what Jacob wanted most. Those sons she bore, Joseph and Benjamin, went on to live out amazing stories of their own, a lasting legacy of her most personal wish.

*L*EAH
(Genesis 29:15–30:21, 31:4–21)

If Rachel was love at first sight for Jacob, Leah was the opposite. She wasn't physically beautiful or attractive in comparison with her younger sister. Even though Leah is the older sister, at the beginning of the story, we see her described only in terms of how she stacks up against Rachel. Rachel was the one who took center stage. Rachel was the one who met Jacob at the well, the one to captivate him. Rachel was the sort of woman men fell in love with at first sight, and Leah, apparently, was not—at least not for Jacob.

> Now Laban had two daughters; the name of the older was Leah, and the name of the younger was Rachel. Leah had weak eyes, but Rachel had a lovely figure and was beautiful. (Genesis 29:16–17)

For centuries, Jewish and Christian scholars alike have puzzled over what this description means. What does it mean for someone to have "weak eyes"? Does it mean that Leah was nearsighted? Possibly, Leah couldn't see very well and squinted a great deal. This might have meant she moved more slowly and awkwardly than the confident, dazzling Rachel. Some scholars interpret the wording to mean her eyes actually appeared younger than Rachel's. In any case, Leah isn't portrayed the way her sister is. In this verse, Rachel is described in the Hebrew as *yifat mareh*, "beautiful of sight."

In the context of the marriage practices of ancient Near Eastern families, it makes sense that these two family units, that of Rebekah and that of Laban, may have been looking to each other. Jacob was forbidden to marry a Canaanite woman, so traveling back to family in Mesopotamia would have been logical. After all, when he was fleeing for his life, his mother, Rebekah, sent him to her brother, Laban. And Rebekah had two sons, while Laban had two daughters. It's possible there was a family understanding regarding an arranged marriage between the sets of cousins, which would have made Esau's decision to marry Canaanite wives all the more irritating to his mother. Rebekah did say to Jacob that if he, too, married one of the Canaanite women, "my life will not be worth living" (Genesis 27:46).

It is also tempting to wonder if Leah was downhearted living in constant comparison to Rachel. Was she viewed her whole life as second-rate in contrast to her beautiful younger sister? We have a hint of this in Laban's double dealing regarding Rachel's wedding. Why would Laban have stooped to this kind of trickery? Were there no takers for Leah? Why didn't Laban explain the custom to Jacob; should Jacob already have known of it? For all his wealth, Laban might have realized that there would be no offers forthcoming for his older daughter, and so he capitalized on Jacob's presence to make sure that Leah, too, had a husband.

How did Leah feel about all this? We don't hear her speak until she names her firstborn son, and then we have a hint:

When the Lord saw that Leah was not loved, he enabled her to conceive, but Rachel remained childless. Leah became pregnant and gave birth to a son. She named him Reuben, for she said, "It is because the Lord has seen my misery. Surely my husband will love me now." (Genesis 29:31–32)

What Leah felt about all this was likely humiliated—humiliated that her younger sister was constantly preferred over her, humiliated that she was able to have a husband only by trickery and deceit—deceit in which she had to actively participate in order to seal her marriage to a man who didn't want her in the first place. Leah's lot was a difficult one, but notice what she says about it: the Lord saw her misery. These words are similar to those of Hagar, who, like Leah, was also rejected. Both of them cried out to a God who truly saw them, almost certainly in a way that no human eyes ever did. Hagar was "unseen" because of her slave status, and Leah felt "unseen" because she felt unloved, or at least less loved than Rachel. But the God who saw Leah knew of her distress and had mercy.

It's worth pausing here and thinking a little about the religious identity of Laban and his family. We know that Abraham and his son Isaac worshipped the one true and living God, who made Himself known in personal revelation to them. Jacob was raised to worship the same God, whom he personally encountered in his vision of the stairway (or ladder) at Bethel. But there is no idea yet in Scripture that people outside this small family circle are worshipping Abraham's God. In fact, we know that Laban had idols, or "images," in his home because Genesis 31 tells us that Rachel stole them. It's likely Rachel and Leah were not raised to worship Abraham's God; at this point in the Bible story, God is unknown to those outside the tight-knit family circle of Abraham's sons and grandsons.

But that circle apparently grew to include Leah, who must

have adopted her husband's God as her own—developing a true and living relationship with Him, a bond that involved conversation. We can imagine her pouring out her sorrows, feeling like an afterthought who couldn't capture her husband's heart no matter how hard she tried, always finishing a distant second place to her stunning sister. What might she have come to know about God in those lonely nights of prayer?

That prayer was answered with the birth of Reuben. Here was Leah, the unloved, the runner-up in the sweepstakes of life, the eternal second best, and yet *she* was the one who produced Jacob's firstborn son and heir. The first syllable of Reuben's name is *Re*, for "look." *Look what God has done for me*, it means, but as Leah herself says, it also means that God looked on her. The name, as Leah understands it, is not about glorifying her, but about her gratefulness to God. And frankly, at this point in the story, Leah must feel so alone—as alone as she has been her whole life. But finally, in her husband's God, she has found something different, someone different, someone who sees not just her but the reality of her situation.

Leah went on to give birth again:

> She conceived again, and when she gave birth to a son she said, "Because the Lord heard that I am not loved, he gave me this one too." So she named him Simeon. (Genesis 29:33)

Simeon's name in Hebrew is "Shimon." The first part of that name, the root word, means "to hear." The God she had come to know and trust had not only *seen* her, but *heard* her. She was completely known. And God's blessings to the unloved Leah continued to be poured out abundantly: Leah had two more sons.

Again she conceived, and when she gave birth to a son she said, "Now at last my husband will become attached to me, because I have borne him three sons." So he was named Levi. She conceived again, and when she gave birth to a son she said, "This time I will praise the Lord." So she named him Judah. Then she stopped having children. (Genesis 29:34–35)

Levi's name means "attached" or "joined," and Leah's hope, heartbreaking as it was, was that Jacob would come to love her as he loved Rachel, and be bonded to her. Even though she bore yet another son after Levi, we don't see that it ever vaulted her past her sister in terms of Jacob's affection. And yet, Leah found reason to praise God.

When her fourth son was born, she gave him an astonishing name: "Yahuda," or "Judah," meaning "Praise to Yah." "Yah" is the ancient name of Abraham's God, less a proper name than an acclamation of love and adoration. She invoked the name of the God whom Jacob had shown her, and she gave thanks to Him. For the first time, in naming her son, she did not reference her external circumstances or her husband's neglect (Reuben: "surely my husband will love me now"; Simon: "the Lord heard I am not loved"; Levi: "Now at last my husband will become attached to me"). Instead, in humble gratitude, she says, "This time I will praise the Lord."

And she made that choice despite some incredibly challenging circumstances. It was clear her husband preferred Rachel to her, all while Rachel was sinking deeper into hatred and resentment of her more fertile sister. This was a highly dysfunctional family. But Leah found a way to focus on the blessings God had given her, not the ones He hadn't. She still wanted Jacob's love, as her choice of the plaintive name "Levi" tells us, but she did not let that desire crush her. God remained the center and foundation of her being. God had given her the blessing of six healthy sons, an incredible richness in the ancient world. Here, in the story of Leah, we see the theme that will appear again and again in Scripture, the story of God's reversal of the world's values. Leah the unloved becomes the beloved of God, and her rejection by her husband becomes the occasion of her abundant blessing.

Slowly, through her journey, we see Leah growing and becoming stronger, surer of herself. In the initial verses of the story, Leah seems to have little to say for herself. Let's be clear: her first words are about her humiliation. She is quiet and retiring, not the kind of person to stand up for herself. But after her sons are born, she is different, and we see that difference unfold gradually.

Rachel's plan to conceive through her slave Bilhah was a strategy that Leah eagerly copied. Leah was practical, and she knew a good idea when she saw one. Don't think she wasn't viewing this as a competition, just as Rachel did. As soon as Rachel had successfully attained two sons through Bilhah, Leah offered up her servant Zilpah. (Imagine the stories we'd hear from Bilhah's and Zilpah's perspectives.) Again, the names Leah gave these sons tell us a great deal about her spiritual state. Rachel gave Bilhah's children names denoting victory and judgment, seeing their birth as one more move in her great contest with her sister. But Leah named Zilpah's boys "Gad" and "Asher," names meaning "good fortune" and "blessing," respectively.

It's worth pausing to reflect on who names the children in the Bible. In almost every instance in the narrative of Genesis, it is the women who do the naming, and this can be viewed as a reflection of their spiritual state—think of Rachel naming her final child "Son of Pain," or Sarah commemorating her laughter in Isaac's name. Fertility and childbearing were deeply spiritual activities, markers not just of social status but of one's relationship with God. The naming of children was a kind of statement for mothers, a way in which women told part of the story of the lineage that created God's people. The names that Leah gave her children reflected both her present circumstances and her hopes for their futures.

By the time we see the sisters bargaining over the mandrakes, Leah is beginning to stand up for herself. We saw some of this passage earlier, but here's a bit more context, to help us better understand:

> During wheat harvest, Reuben went out into the fields and found some mandrake plants, which he brought to his mother Leah. Rachel said to Leah, "Please give me some of your son's mandrakes." But she said to her, "Wasn't it enough that you took away my husband? Will you take my son's mandrakes too?" "Very well," Rachel said, "he can sleep with you tonight in return for your son's mandrakes." (Genesis 30:14–15)

If we wondered before if Leah was aware of the ongoing competition with her sister, we see clearly here that she was. And if Rachel's grief was her barrenness, Leah's grief in feeling rejected and disregarded was equally poignant. She wanted her husband to love her. Leah says a lot in that very revealing comment about how Rachel "took away" her husband. She had had

Jacob fully to herself for only a week. Remember, while Jacob had agreed to serve another seven years in exchange for Rachel, he married the younger sister only one week after he married Leah (Genesis 29:27–28). Was there part of Leah that thought that Jacob might have come to love her fully in time if the beautiful Rachel hadn't been on the scene? Or, worse, did she wonder if her husband and her sister openly discussed his preference for Rachel over her? A woman who had spent so much of her life rejected and unloved was bound to wonder if her rival and her husband were quietly snickering at her some nights. The thought of never being enough must have tormented her, and both she and Rachel found ways to pour out their grief and anger at each other.

Shy, retiring Leah appears to be gone by the time we get to the mandrake story. She was the mother of five sons, the unquestioned matriarch of their family group. She did not hesitate to bite back at Rachel, and she did not hesitate to give orders to Jacob, who apparently complied without question. We see her son Reuben's devotion to her in his offering to her of the rare and valuable mandrake roots he has found. Slowly, we see a picture of Leah emerging: a loving mother, but a woman who is now unafraid to bargain for and assert her rights, a woman who knew what she was worth in God's eyes even if her husband never put her first.

It's a sure bet that at some point in Leah's life, she imagined how happy and peaceful her life could have been if Rachel had married someone else and gone far away. In time, Jacob might have forgotten about her and come to love Leah. Leah's married life could have been harmonious, and when she bore children, they would not have been one more thing for her sister to resent.

Leah might have wanted an escape from the never-ending contest with her sister. But the truth is, without that relationship, Leah might never have become the calm, confident woman of God she clearly is by the end of the narrative.

How often do we think, *How much easier would my life be without this irritating person in it?* We might even speculate about the peace and success we could achieve if only so-and-so would stop making it hard for us. But the Rachels in our lives, the people who force us to deal with difficult circumstances, can also be the ones who push us into a deeper relationship with God. Can we turn those struggles with the Rachels in our lives into a truly vulnerable, more profound relationship with the God who understands it all? Can we go as far as Leah and praise God in our circumstances, even when we feel unloved and invisible?

Though Leah may not ever have received her husband's love, she most certainly received God's blessing. Through her son Levi came Moses, Aaron, and Miriam and all the priests of Israel. Her son Judah became a great prince and gave his name not only to the entire southern half of the kingdom of Israel, Judea, but also to the People of the Book, the Jews. Judah was also the ancestor of King David. Indeed, Leah was the mother of the entire royal line of Israel, the mother of kings and princes for a thousand years. And of course, she was also the sister who appears in the lineage of Christ, who Himself descended through David from Leah's son Judah. Jesus was the Lion of Judah, the true king of Israel.

We get a lovely picture of redemption through Leah, because the greatest member of the nation of Israel ever to be born, Christ our Savior, was the child of the lesser-loved wife. Leah knew what it was to be rejected, a sorrow Jesus also knew. He was despised and mocked. He warned His disciples that He would "suffer many things and be rejected by this generation" (Luke 17:25). God Himself has inhabited the grief of rejection. That Jesus came to this world through Leah's offspring is a wonderful picture: God waits for us not only in the places of beauty and popularity, but also often in the places of brokenness and rejection, the darkest valleys and the ugliest messes. There we find God deeply present, seeing our misery and bringing us our most precious blessing, just as He did for His daughter Leah.

Rachel and Leah Study Questions

1. The whole story is governed by Jacob's choice of Rachel over Leah. What happens to the relationship between Rachel and Leah because of Jacob?

2. Choice is a recurring theme throughout the story of the three of them: Jacob, Rachel, and Leah. In what ways does Jacob make choices? Look at Genesis 27:19 and the verses that follow, in which Jacob chooses to deceive his father; Genesis 29:18, when Jacob chooses Rachel; and Genesis 31:1–13, when Jacob chooses to leave Laban. Is there a common thread in his choices? In the last choice he makes, he now has both Rachel and Leah with him. How is that choice different from the first two choices, which he makes on his own?

3. In what ways does Rachel make choices? Look at Genesis 30:1–8. What choice is she making here, and what is driving her? Leah makes choices, too: look at the verses that follow, in Genesis 30:9–21.

4. The sisters make a choice together in Genesis 31:14–16. Why do they choose their husband over their father, and what lies behind that choice? What has Laban done to drive them to that choice?

   The story of the three of them shows us that often, when we think we are making a free choice, we are really just reacting to something else. What is an example of a choice in your own life that you later realized was not as "free" as you thought it was?

5. Why is it that God appears so little in this story? In the stories of Jacob's grandfather Abraham and his father, Isaac, God takes center stage. Why does God seem to recede into the background in the story of Jacob? What might be going on there?

Take a look at the reunion between Jacob and Esau in Genesis 34. What does Jacob mean when he says to Esau, "[F]or to see your face is like seeing the face of God"? What does this imply about human relationships in the Jacob/Rachel/Leah story?

TAMAR AND RUTH

Outsiders

TAMAR
(Genesis 38:1–30)

When we look for inspiring women in the Bible, Tamar's story is not exactly the first one that comes to mind. It's strange and uncomfortable, and Tamar makes choices that, let's face it, can in no way be explained to a children's Sunday school class. So, her story tends to remain a footnote, one we might quickly move past in search of material that's easier to understand and a character who is perhaps easier to relate to.

But to fast-forward past her would be a shame, because Tamar is a fascinating woman with a story we need to hear. She's an outsider, not part of the family made up of Abraham's descendants who will become the nation of Israel. Nevertheless, she is part of both David and Jesus's family tree. She's also an example of bold choices and of God's redemptive power in the midst of our messy lives.

Her story appears in a kind of interlude in the story of Genesis, and that placement is important. The previous chapter is the beginning of the story of Joseph; it ends with the selling of Joseph into slavery by his envious brothers. The Bible tells us that selling him is Judah's idea and, in Genesis 37:11, that "his brothers were jealous of him"—and with good reason! They were all sons of Jacob, but Joseph was the firstborn son of the wife Jacob truly loved, Rachel. Genesis 37:3 doesn't beat around the bush, telling us that Jacob "loved Joseph more than any of his other sons." So, was Judah looking for a way to get rid of Joseph for good? Or was he looking to avert a worse fate? Both? The brothers' original intention was to kill Joseph, but Reuben convinced them to abandon their deadly plan. By suggesting that the brothers sell Joseph to a passing caravan of Midianites, was Judah hoping to save Joseph from his bloodthirsty brothers? Or was Judah in fact the ringleader?

Immediately after Joseph is sold into slavery, Judah left his brothers and went to live among the Canaanites. He married a Canaanite woman and had three sons by her. He built a life there, away from his father's family. His sons grew up, and eventually he acquired a wife for his oldest son, Er. But Er was, apparently, no good. Scripture tells us simply that he "was wicked in the Lord's sight" (Genesis 38:7).

It's at this point that Tamar enters the picture. She was the wife of Er, likely married to him as a teenager. Imagine her situation: a very young woman, given in marriage to a foreigner through no choice of her own, living in an unfamiliar culture with a husband so wicked that God decides to kill him.

After Er's death, custom dictated that his wife be married to his brother. This is known as a "leviratic" marriage—*levir* is Latin for "husband's brother"—and it was the custom among many Semitic peoples of the ancient Near East. It later became enshrined as part of Jewish law in the Torah. The idea behind it is a simple one: if a married man died without leaving behind any sons, it was the duty of his brother to marry the widow and have sons with her—sons that would be counted as the dead brother's heirs. It was a way of affirming that the dead continued to live and be part of the community they'd left behind. And initially, at least, Judah followed this custom. He dutifully gave Tamar in marriage to his second son, Onan. Apparently, Onan was not a fan of the arrangement. There is a selflessness in leviratic marriage, because the male partner has to be willing to recognize the first-born son he produces with his brother's widow as the heir of his deceased brother and not his own. Onan apparently was not so willing. He went through with the marriage in public, but in private, he practiced an early form of birth control that meant Tamar would never conceive a son. As the remaining eldest son of Judah, Onan was likely calculating the economic cost of producing an heir for Er. That son would take a portion of the inheritance that would otherwise go to Onan. Fully aware of Onan's selfishness, both physically and economically, God struck him down, too.

It's at this point that Judah apparently decided that Tamar's seeming barrenness was not the result of the wickedness or selfishness of his own children—it was Tamar. *She* must be the problem. So, he sent her back home to her father's house, making an excuse about his youngest son, Shelah, not being old enough yet to enter into a marriage with her. In reality, Judah had no intention of letting her within ten miles of yet another son of his, leviratic custom or no. Genesis 38:11 tells us exactly what Judah was thinking: "He may die too, just like his brothers." What choice did Tamar have but to obey, and trust that Judah would eventually do the right thing?

The Bible tells us that Tamar went to dwell in her father's house but not how she felt about any of this. We don't know if she loved Er, or how she felt about Onan. Maybe she never loved them; she would not have been consulted. Marriage was something arranged by men, a business deal to be struck, like the sale of goats or land. And if Tamar was a business deal, then she had just gone bankrupt. Twice a widow, she now waited to see if her father-in-law would make good on his implication that she would one day become Shelah's wife.

The news of Tamar's bad luck had probably spread; most likely there were whispered rumors and quiet chuckles inside tents about the woman who was so devastatingly unlucky. An object of ridicule, Tamar must have felt the label, too, a fatal plague that no one would want to contract.

It would have been easy for Tamar to say, *Well, they must be right about me. I must truly be worthless, and maybe Judah is right, maybe it really is all my fault that his sons died.* Like Job, she could have sat on a dung heap and wailed about how her life had turned out—no marriage, no future, no prospects of any kind of normal life, but being a dependent in her father's house until the day she died. But that's not what she did. She didn't lose sight of the fact that it was Judah who had done the wrong thing. So, she formulated a plan.

Here is where the story goes off the Sunday school rails, because after realizing that Judah has no plans to join her in marriage with his son Shelah, Tamar decided to trick Judah into sleeping with her. She took off the distinctive clothing of a widow, wrapped herself in a veil, and journeyed to a place where she knew Judah would pass on his travels.

Tamar's face was obscured so that her father-in-law wouldn't recognize her. Assuming she was a prostitute, Judah, who himself had become a widower at this point, said, "Come now, let me sleep with you." She accepted, but drove a hard bargain—he would have to leave his signet ring, cord, and staff until he could return with payment. These details (especially the jewelry) tell us just how wealthy Judah must have been. They give us a glimpse of the power he had—in stark contrast to Tamar's lowly position. More important, such items in those days were a form of identification, the closest Tamar would come to having DNA proof when she needed it.

Once they had slept together, Tamar took her father-in-law's ring, cord, and staff and left before he could recognize her. Judah did try to find her later, sending a friend to deliver the payment and get his things back, but she had vanished. The friend even asked around about her—*Hey, what about that prostitute who sits by the side of the road here?*—but no one had ever heard of such a woman, and Judah was worried he could become a "laughingstock" (Genesis 38:23) if he pressed the issue.

Three months later, Tamar, now pregnant, was so far along that it could no longer be concealed. Judah was outraged. Genesis 38:24 documents his reaction: "Bring her out and have her burned to death!" In sending her away from his home, Judah had effectively repudiated her, and he would have been happy never to hear from her again—until she publicly embarrassed him with a pregnancy. He had been happy to ignore her, until now. Now, suddenly, he cared a lot about what she did and how she made him look. Remember, he was still responsible for her. People must have been whispering, *Isn't that the woman who was . . . Yes, to Judah's sons! Oh, poor Judah.* The snickers in the tents started up again. Judah was publicly humiliated, and he wanted to make Tamar pay for it even if that meant putting her to death for making the exact same error he himself had made just a few months before.

Tamar sent him an unmistakable message, delivering his signet ring, cord, and staff.

> As she was being brought out, she sent a message to her father-in-law. "I am pregnant by the man who owns these," she said. And she added, "See if you recognize whose seal and cord and staff these are." (Genesis 38:25)

In those times, these items truly would have equated to a paternity test, holding a mirror up to a man's actions. Judah could not deny that they were his. Did he erupt in fury? Did he double down on his resolve to burn Tamar to death, so that no one would ever know of his mistake or his hypocrisy?

He did none of those things. Instead, bowing his head and acknowledging the justice of her reproof, he made a remarkable admission:

> "She is more righteous than I, since I wouldn't give her to my son Shelah." (Genesis 38:26)

Some translate the Hebrew as simply, "She is righteous; I am not." Judah recognized that the root of the whole tangle was his own decision not to let Tamar marry Shelah. Yes, she behaved immorally, but what if he had dealt justly with her from the beginning? Judah at last admitted that he was the root of the problem, not Tamar.

It's a remarkable moment, and it calls to mind another moment when a man of God sins and is called to account for it. In 2 Samuel 12, the prophet Nathan appears before David to confront him for murdering Uriah and sleeping with Uriah's wife, Bathsheba. Like Judah, David didn't explode in rage. He listened, stricken to the heart, and fell at the prophet's feet in repentance. Judah's repentance was even more remarkable, though, because it was not a mighty and well-respected prophet who reproached him, but a woman. A woman! A woman pregnant outside marriage, no less. He could have brushed her aside and had her killed, along with her unborn child. But he listened, bowed his head, and admitted that she was right and he was wrong.

Tamar, a woman with no power, no standing in her community, and no male protector looking out for her, delivered a powerful rebuke to Judah, and was heard. We can imagine what she must have felt, being escorted into his presence for the first time since their fateful meeting of three months before. Did Judah bow his head before her, the mother of his unborn child? Was she feeling vindicated?

It would have been easy for Tamar to wait to be brought into Judah's presence and there, publicly, to announce the truth. After all, wasn't that what Judah deserved, some good old-fashioned public humiliation? It would have been such a moment of triumph for her. Imagine all the mocking and contempt that had been heaped on her all those years now heaped on Judah instead. What a tempting thought that must have been. But Tamar chose a different path. She had a message sent privately to him instead. She chose *not* to publicly humiliate the man who was trying to have her executed. She invited him to connect the dots and then awaited his decision. The sequence of events reminds us that seeking justice doesn't require humiliation; we can advocate for what is rightfully ours without destroying others in the process.

Tamar's significance did not end with that moment of truth. She went on to give birth to twin boys, Perez and Zerah. These sons of Judah had an important role to play in salvation history. In the first chapter of the Gospel of Matthew, we read the genealogy of Jesus. "Abraham begot Isaac," read the familiar words, "Isaac begot Jacob, and Jacob begot Judah and his brothers. Judah begot Perez and Zerah by Tamar. Perez begot Hezron, and Hezron begot Ram" (Matthew 1:2–3). Ram was the great-great-great-great-great-grandfather of King David, and so Tamar's little boy—son of an outsider, son of a Canaanite woman—became part of the royal line of the kingdom of Israel. Tamar's name was even invoked in a special blessing we'll see in our next story (Ruth 4:12). But this was the genealogy not just of David, but of David's divine descendant, Jesus. Tamar is part of that lineage and is one of only three women named in Matthew's genealogy. Tamar helps make the Messiah possible, and this non-Jewish Canaanite outsider who was pregnant out of wedlock and faced a certain death became the ancestress of Christ.

Tamar's story has significance within the narrative of Genesis, too. Remember that her story happens in the middle of Joseph's story. The narrative suddenly pauses to give us this seemingly random interlude with Judah and Tamar. Joseph's story picks back up immediately after the birth of Perez and Zerah, continuing without interruption for the rest of the Book of Genesis. At first glance, it makes no sense to find this illicit story shoehorned into Joseph's. What does this sordid tale have to do with anything?

Judah gives us a clue.

When Joseph was thrown into the empty pit by his blood-thirsty brothers, it was Judah who came up with the idea to sell him away. It was Judah who said, *Let's get rid of him.* But at the conclusion of the story, when Joseph's frail elderly father, Jacob, faces the possibility of sending his beloved son Benjamin away into Egypt, it is Judah who steps forward.

> Then Judah said to [Jacob] his father, "Send the boy along with me and we will go at once, so that we and you and our children may live and not die. I myself will guarantee his safety; you can hold me personally responsible for him. If I do not bring him back to you and set him here before you, I will bear the blame before you all my life." (Genesis 43:8–9)

When they arrived in Egypt, the worst appeared to have happened. The capricious governor (in reality, their brother Joseph in disguise) demanded that they leave the hapless young Benjamin with him. Judah put his own life on the line: "Take me instead of him," he pled with the governor (Genesis 44:33), offering his own life for his brother's. It was Judah who had grown and changed the most of all the brothers—but why? What explains the change from the angry, vengeful young man of the beginning of the story to the mature, compassionate man at the end? Was it his humbling before Tamar? Tamar's actions forced Judah to confront his own wrongdoing. Probably for the first time, Judah learned what it was to say in public, *I was wrong.* Tamar showed him the way of righteousness and how to be a person who stands for right when no one else has the courage.

There is an ancient Jewish tradition that says that to publicly

shame another person is the same as committing murder because, regardless of your reasons, you have murdered that person's reputation forever. It is the sort of teaching that reminds us
to be careful with our words. But which of us, in Tamar's shoes,
could have resisted the temptation to make sure Judah got a little of what was coming to him?

Tamar's story is a beautiful illustration of how God can redeem even the most ill-advised human plans. Tamar likely felt
abandoned and may have had many different motivations: justice, desperation, an attempt at preserving the life she thought
she was going to create. But hadn't she seen God deal with wrong-
doers in the past? It cost both her husbands their lives. A widow
seducing her father-in-law in order to become pregnant seems
like an irredeemable plan at first blush, but God is masterful at
making good out of our messes. Tamar's story is woven into the
fabric of the lineage of Jesus Christ. No matter how unfaithful
we may be, God is always working in each of our stories, able not
only to heal us, but also to use our human frailty to miraculous
ends.

ℛUTH
(Ruth 1:1–4:22)

Many of us are familiar with the story of Ruth. After all, Ruth is something of a superstar—a woman who has her own book in the Bible! In fact, Ruth is the only non-Jewish woman to have a book of the Bible named after her.

Ruth is marked as an outsider from the very beginning of her story. Like Tamar, she wasn't a descendant of Abraham. She was a woman of Moab, the land on the eastern shore of the Dead Sea, across from Judea. She married a young Jewish man named Mahlon, whose family had fled a disastrous famine in Judea and gone looking for a better life elsewhere. But tragedy followed the family. Her father-in-law, Elimelech, died shortly after the family arrived in Moab. Sometime after that, both her husband and his brother, Kilion, also died. Along with her sister-in-law Orpah and her mother-in-law, Naomi, Ruth became part of a grieving trio: three women bound together in heartbreak, with limited prospects for the future.

The famine in Judea having ended, Naomi decided to do what many of us would probably do in that situation: she chose to head for home. Her two daughters-in-law began the journey with her. After all, who did the three women have but one another? But Naomi wouldn't hear of it. She urged the two young women to go back to their own homelands and try again. After all, they were young! They could marry again, which would give them renewed hope for family and children. Orpah agreed, but not Ruth. The first words Ruth said in this tragically beautiful story constitute a declaration of such breathtaking love and loyalty that they are still used today as an expression of ultimate devotion:

> "Don't urge me to leave you or to turn back from you. Where you go I will go, and where you stay I will stay. Your people will be my people and your God my God. Where you die I will die, and there I will be buried." (Ruth 1:16–17a)

You've likely heard these stirring words before, but think about what this really meant for Ruth. She was completely disavowing her former life and pledging to commit to a new country, a new home, a new people, even a new religious affiliation. It's truly remarkable.

So, together, Ruth and Naomi journeyed to Naomi's home country of Judea and to her home city of Bethlehem. Here is where an observant reader will sit up and take notice, because this is the first mention of Bethlehem in the Bible. To an ancient Jew reading this story, the significance of the city is obvious: this is the city of David's birth, the home of the great king. But to a Christian reading this story, the city is much more than the home of an earthly king: it is the birthplace of the eternal king, Jesus. Ancient Christian writers associated the Hebrew meaning of the city's name, "House of Bread," with Jesus, the "true bread from heaven." Bethlehem is where the whole salvation story begins, so, as Christians reading this story, we know to pay attention. Everything that Bethlehem will come to mean for us begins right here, when a grieving immigrant woman follows her mother-in-law into a strange city.

The decision to create a new family despite the lack of a blood connection is an important one, and it's a theme this story returns to again and again. So much of the Bible's narrative is focused on biological family and the importance of having one's own children. It's what drives Sarah and Rachel and, as we will see later in these pages, Hannah and countless other men and women in the Bible to fall on their faces before God in prayer, begging for children of their own. Throughout the Old Testament, children are often viewed as the single greatest blessing. And we have the Book of Ruth showing us that even when that option seems out of reach, God is always weaving together the unexpected. Ruth and Naomi are a family—a family formed by Ruth's selfless choice. And by the end of the story, their love will have expanded outward to create even more family and Ruth will eventually be hailed as "better to you than seven sons." But we're not there yet.

When Ruth and Naomi arrived in Bethlehem, they were destitute. Ruth joined in doing what the poor of that time and region did, which was to gather up the scraps of barley left in the field after the reapers had moved through. Every field must have had impoverished people just like them hanging on to its margins, waiting for a few stray stalks of grain to fall. In Leviticus 19:9-10, we see God's directive to leave the edges of fields unharvested in order to help the impoverished. After a while, maybe the local people got used to seeing Ruth the same way those of us who live in cities take the presence of the urban poor for granted. How often do our eyes glaze over at the approach of a dirty, shabby panhandler? If we think of them at all, do we wonder, before quickly looking away, if their own bad choices led them there?

Boaz was one of those wealthy landowners, a close relative of Naomi. But to him, the poor gleaners were not invisible. He saw a new face among them and asked who she was. When he found out that this was the loyal young woman who journeyed to Bethlehem with Naomi, he insisted that she be given a protected place among the female gleaners and that she be allowed water along with the reapers. This was counter to the culture in numerous ways: Boaz was giving a foreigner, a *woman*, preferential treatment. Ruth was astonished at this generosity and asked Boaz why on earth he would show her such gracious favor. Boaz's answer was simple: he was kind to Ruth because he had heard of her humble kindness. In Ruth 2, we find yet another passage of compassionate words when they are needed most. Boaz says to Ruth:

> "I've been told all about what you have done for your mother-in-law since the death of your husband—how you left your father and mother and your homeland and came to live with a people you did not know before. May the Lord repay you for what you have done. May you be richly rewarded by the Lord, the God of Israel, under whose wings you have come to take refuge." (Ruth 2:11-12)

Scripture often shows us God favoring those willing to leave everything for His sake. What was the very first command God gave Abraham? "Go from your country, your people and your father's household," God said, "to the land I will show you" (Genesis 12:1). It's as if God sometimes has to pry us out of our comfort zones before He can accomplish His purposes through us. We often need to be jostled into a radical dependence on God before we can make real spiritual progress.

When Naomi found out about Boaz's extraordinary kindness

to Ruth, she hatched a plan: Ruth's marriage to him. After all, Boaz was a relative of Naomi's husband, which made him a kinsman to her daughter-in-law as well. In this position, Boaz could act as a kinsman-redeemer, someone willing to marry a kinsman's widow and restore her position in the family. Marrying the wealthy Boaz would have been a life-changing event for an impoverished immigrant like Ruth.

Naomi's plan seemed sound, but it all depended on Boaz's consent, and he could have several reasons to say no. For one thing, as we saw in the story of Tamar, marrying a woman only to have her son not "count" as your own for inheritance purposes was a difficult, selfless choice. Most men wanted their "own" wife with their "own" children, who would inherit their property and carry on their name. That aside, why would Boaz marry a woman who was a stranger in his country? She had no powerful family connections who could help him professionally, and there would be no advantage to him at all in such a match. He had every legitimate reason to refuse.

Maybe the next part of Naomi's plan was intended to give Boaz an out, if he wanted one. Ruth, a humble woman, was careful not to put Boaz in an embarrassing public situation. During this joyful time of harvest, Boaz was sleeping on the threshing room floor with his men, likely after a party celebrating the harvest. Ruth 3:7 tells us that "Boaz had finished eating and drinking and was in good spirits." He stretched out near a heap of grain and closed his eyes to relax, satisfied with a good day's work. Following Naomi's plan, Ruth crept in, silently curled up at his feet, and waited. She waited all night long. Was she nervous, anxiously watching for any sign that Boaz was stirring and would soon find her there, or was her heart at peace given that she was in the presence of a man who had already shown her incredible kindness?

What would Boaz do when he woke up and found her there? He was kind to her in broad daylight, when other people were watching. Would he be different in the dark, where she alone would be privy to his momentous decision? She was a stranger, an immigrant, a Gentile, an outsider. Naomi considered her family, but that didn't actually make her a blood relative. Boaz had no obligation to her, not really. So, what did Boaz say when he awoke and found her there?

> "The Lord bless you, my daughter," he replied. "This kindness is greater than that which you showed earlier: You have not run after the younger men, whether rich or poor. And now, my daughter, don't be afraid. I will do for you all you ask. All the people of my town know that you are a woman of noble character." (Ruth 3:10–11)

Against all odds, Ruth found security and happiness. Boaz responded to the nobility of her nature. He was clearly deeply impressed by her. He married her, but not before another interesting twist, one that returns us once again to the theme of choice. Another (unnamed) male relative of Naomi's had first right of refusal of Naomi's property and her daughter-in-law. It would be a choice with lifelong consequences. Boaz alerted the man to a piece of land belonging to the late Elimelech, a parcel Naomi hoped to sell. Though the man was interested in the land, when Boaz revealed that its sale would be contingent upon his taking Ruth in marriage, he declined. "Then I cannot redeem it because I might endanger my own estate," he says in Ruth 4:6.

Who knows what eventually came of that man. We don't even know his name because he glides out of the story of salvation unknown forever. He passed on marrying Ruth—Ruth, the ancestor of King David, Ruth the ancestor of Christ Himself! He chose another path. And Boaz chose Ruth.

Brave and momentous choices are everywhere in this story. Naomi's husband, Elimelech, left his homeland and made a new life for himself in Moab. Naomi chose to return home after his death. Ruth made the most daring choice of all, leaving her home and family to follow Naomi into the unknown. And Boaz could have rejected Ruth just like the nameless kinsman did, but he didn't. He married her, and together they built a new family. Naomi, Ruth, and Boaz built a family of choice, a family that branched into the tree of life that bears our Savior.

Early Christians, when they read the story of Ruth, couldn't help but see themselves in it. For them, it was more than just a nice story about a young woman who got her happy ending. Ruth's acceptance into the family of Israel spoke to them about their own inclusion in God's family. They found in this story an echo of Paul's words about the Gentile church, the "wild olive tree, grafted in among them, and with them . . . a partaker of the root and fat of the olive tree" (Romans 11:17).

Ruth chose to leave her people and her gods, just as the Gentile people chose to leave theirs. Like Ruth, they, too, came to the "House of Bread," Bethlehem, hungry for any scraps they could find. And like her, they found themselves the unexpected recipients of the fullness of the promise. Ruth (like Abraham) became a powerful symbol of the riches that await those who choose to step out in faith and who leave behind the comfortable in favor of the strange and spiritually challenging.

Christian writers also found an echo of Jesus in the way Ruth was treated. She arrived in Bethlehem expecting to be regarded as the least of the least. But Boaz never saw her that way. He called her blessed and told her not to fear. When she lay prostrate at his feet, he lifted her up like the father of the Prodigal Son and celebrated her. Boaz brought her unexpected blessings and favored her. Is it any wonder that Christians see in him a reflection of the love of Christ for His Gentile church? Ruth's story strikes a powerful emotional chord in Gentile readers who see themselves in it.

For ancient readers, life was not full of the kinds of choices we have. Part of the power of Ruth's story lies in the idea that it is a *woman* making these choices. Choices for everyone were much more constrained in Ruth's time, but women's choices were practically nonexistent. Today we take for granted that women in much of the world can choose what they want to do with their lives, what they will study and where they will go to school, even whom they will marry. These are elementary choices that define basic freedom in our culture. But none of these freedoms were readily available to the women we are reading about, and they certainly weren't available to Ruth. So, for Ruth to make such a radical choice—leaving her home country without any male protection and following Naomi to Judea—would have been almost unbelievable to early readers. Her decision to do so would have underscored the power of her determination and the importance of choice in their own lives.

So, why did Ruth do it? That is the question lurking at the heart of this story. The Bible does not give us a definitive answer. Some interpreters theorize that Ruth was making a religious statement—perhaps the years she spent as Mahlon's wife and in a Jewish family had convinced her that the God of Israel was the only true god and the one she wanted to follow, too. Others believe Ruth's choice was an ethical and moral one. If she had chosen not to journey with Naomi back to Bethlehem, Naomi, an elderly woman, would have had to travel alone. Ruth's act of kindness may have preserved Naomi's life. Boaz certainly seems to see her actions in this light.

But might there be a lesson in the unknowns? Think about how often we get caught up in worrying about motivations—our own or someone else's. *What did she really mean by that? What's his angle?* First Samuel 16:7 tells us that:

> "God *sees* not as man sees, for man looks at the outward appearance, but the Lord looks at the heart."

God alone knows all that motivated Ruth, but in perfect grace and mercy, her story led to redemption, hope, and the legacy of Jesus Himself.

When Boaz married Ruth, the elders of Bethlehem uttered a blessing upon the two of them:

> May the Lord make the woman who is coming to your house like Rachel and Leah, who together built the house of Israel and wrought mightily in Ephratah. She will have a name in Bethlehem. And out of the seed which the Lord will give you from this young woman, may your house be like the house of Perez, whom Tamar bore to Judah. (Ruth 4:11–12)

What a remarkable statement. Here at the end of the story of Ruth, the Bible specifically points us back to the story of Tamar, inviting us to see these two women in relation to each other.

Because, of course, Tamar was the sixth great-grandmother of Boaz himself and the founding mother (through Judah) of his house. The elders of the city were asking that Boaz's family share in the fruitfulness and stability of the house of Perez, and it's tempting to see something more in that as well. The story of Tamar and Judah was also one of choice. Tamar gave Judah the opportunity, and he did the right thing. Boaz was also given an opportunity by Ruth, and he, too, followed her lead.

The bold moves of Tamar and Ruth caused a kind of chain reaction around them, inspiring choices that ultimately shaped history. Naomi's nameless relative is consigned to scriptural oblivion because he doesn't step up when opportunity comes calling. Maybe he was unprepared or simply not part of God's bigger plan. Each of us, though, must listen and be willing when His unexpected call comes into our lives. Both Tamar and Ruth were outsiders, women "grafted in" to the house of Israel. They stood outside the community of covenant. And yet their actions guaranteed the continuance of the covenant. As Matthew says in his Gospel, when he names both Tamar and Ruth in the genealogy of Christ, the two women were key to the lineage that brought Jesus to earth. God didn't work miracles through them *despite* who they were, but precisely *because* of it.

Jesus issued a warning to the comfortable of His own day when he told the Pharisees that "out of these stones God can raise up children for Abraham" (Matthew 3:9). The family of God is not built on blood, but on choice—God's adoption of us, which we have done nothing to deserve, but also our decision to choose God.

Finally, the presence of Tamar and Ruth in the genealogy of Jesus points us to the value and worth of the work of women—especially in a world that did not always see that value. Ruth bore Boaz a son, and the women of Bethlehem rejoiced with Naomi.

The women said to Naomi: "Praise be to the Lord, who this day has not left you without a guardian-redeemer. May he become famous throughout Israel! He will renew your life and sustain you in your old age. For your daughter-in-law, who loves you and who is better to you than seven sons, has given him birth." (Ruth 4:14–15)

What a shocking statement this must have been to ancient readers! A woman better than sons? A woman who wasn't even related by blood better than seven sons? But a Christian reader finds in these words not just the glad rejoicing of Naomi, who has at last found peace, happiness, and love, but also the faint, far-off glimmer of the kingdom of Christ. In the kingdom we see dawning here, the last will be first and the first will be last, the despised and rejected will be the guests of greatest honor, and many will come from east and west and sit down with Abraham, Isaac, and Jacob—and Ruth and Tamar—in the kingdom of heaven.

Tamar and Ruth Study Questions

1. The stories of Tamar and Ruth both have to do with intermarrying, the marriage of a Jew to a non-Jew. Given what we know about the history of the people of Israel as the Bible tells it to us, why was marrying outside of Israel seen as bad?

2. Look at Numbers 25 and the story of Phinehas, the grandson of Aaron. What is it that Phinehas does? Read Psalm 106:28–31 and the record of Phinehas's actions there. Why is Phinehas so celebrated in the Bible? What threat did he prevent? How is that threat reversed in the cases of Tamar and Ruth?

3. The only sons of Jacob we learn anything personal about are Joseph and Judah. Both the Joseph story and the Judah story feature women involved in illicit sexual activity—Potiphar's wife in the case of Joseph (Genesis 39:1–23) and Tamar in the case of Judah (Genesis 38:1–30). Even though both these women engage in questionable activity, what are the differences between them? How does the Bible portray them differently? What changes do the women work in Joseph and Judah?

4. Ruth's remarkable story shows us so much of what is best in humanity—Ruth's loyalty, Naomi's devotion, Boaz's generosity and kindness. In it, the actions of good people are rewarded. The story is set in the time of biblical judges, and we know from the Book of

Judges, which immediately precedes Ruth, what a violent period this was in Israel's history. Most of the stories in Judges are of human beings at their worst. Why would Ruth's have been an important story to tell? God makes no direct appearance in the story. Where is He in Ruth's story?

Women of Valor

DEBORAH
(Judges 4:1–5:31)

The Book of Judges is a challenging one, in part because it shows the reality of God's children wandering away from His truths, from His promises. It's a hard book to digest because up until now, we've already seen such amazing victories and blessings. God provided a way for the Israelites to conquer and enter their promised land. He knocked down the walls of Jericho before them. He gave them their share in a land flowing with milk and honey. He renewed His covenant with them forever, and they swore to follow Him and His laws to the end of time and beyond.

Wouldn't it be nice to end the story there, to witness the people of Israel remaining as devoted to God as they had been in the joyous time following the Exodus, or as they were at the moment of their triumph at Jericho? But the story of the people of Israel is also our story, and we know that our spiritual lives don't work that way. It's simply not possible to live all our days in the space of those "mountaintop" moments. As the daily demands of life press in on all sides, we can forget just how closely we walked with God in the midst of our toughest challenges, how faithful He has always been and how much we need to cling to His integrity and His promises. The world is constantly trying to lure us away with something else, with temporary fixes that take our eyes off God's steady goodness. Let's face it, just like the Israelites, we're all guilty of becoming untethered from the One who has always been and always will be.

The Book of Judges is the account of that wandering, the story of how Israel had all the gifts God could possibly give it and squandered them. It's also a reminder that God was always there, always giving the Israelites chances to come back, always showing them the path home—just as he does for us today. Each time the people strayed and wound up being oppressed at the hands of their enemies, God provided a judge to give them leadership and guidance, to point them toward repentance and deliverance.

Whenever the Lord raised up a judge for them, he was with the judge and saved them out of the hands of their enemies as long as the judge lived; for the Lord relented because of their groaning under those who oppressed and afflicted them. (Judges 2:18)

One of the guiding stars God offers His people in the Book of Judges is His prophetess Deborah. I have to tell you, she's one of my favorites. For me, the words of her story leap off the pages of my Bible. I find her brave and inspiring, and I'm pretty sure I would have followed her into battle. This was a woman with guts *and* wisdom, a role model for the ages.

In the pages of the Bible, we see women playing all sorts of roles and living rich, complex lives. But it's not often that we see a woman as a war leader, much less the sole authority of an entire nation. Deborah took up the mantle of governance and led her nation to victory in the midst of some very dark days. Her name means "bee"—and how appropriate! She stung her enemies but brought sweetness and refreshment like honey to her people.

When we meet Deborah, the people of Israel are under the thumb of Jabin, one of the Canaanite kings. Jabin's top military commander, Sisera, had "nine hundred chariots of iron," which means he outmatched the children of Israel militarily by a mile. It wasn't even close.

A word about all the chariots: for a people in the remote hill country of Israel, acquiring the materials to build chariots would have required trade. The metal and the skill needed to make a sturdy war chariot would have meant their trading with one of the bigger powers: Egypt or Syria or even local kingdoms like Moab and Edom. Chariots (like the horses necessary to drive them) implied wealth, and connection with the great cities. Israel didn't have either of those. So, the thought of Israel going into battle against a heavily fortified force like Jabin's would have seemed ludicrous.

That's the context in which Deborah arose:

Now Deborah, a prophetess, the wife of Lappidoth, was judging Israel at that time. She used to sit under the palm of Deborah between Ramah and Bethel in the hill country of Ephraim; and the people of Israel came up to her for judgment. (Judges 4:4–5)

The office of judge required more than just the handing down of pronouncements in legal disputes. At the time, it was viewed as a spiritual role as well, and most certainly a position of leadership. The people would have come to Deborah for the settlement of any difficult questions or cases, probably everything from property disputes to homicides. As the nation's leading authority, Deborah (like Moses) was expected to rule on various civil matters. She guided her people in more than one way. She was so famous in ages to come that the writer of Judges called the tree she sat under "the palm of Deborah." Think of how many generations the people of Israel must have kept that place in loving remembrance of one of their bravest and most unique leaders.

Deborah saw the dire situation of her people and decided to act at God's direction. She summoned the warrior Barak, the son of Abinoam, delivered some truth straight from the Source, and she didn't sugarcoat it. She didn't say to him, *I really need your help here.* Deborah spoke with authority: "The Lord, the God of Israel, commands you, 'Go, gather your men at Mount Tabor, taking ten thousand from the tribe of Naphtali and ten thousand from the tribe of Zebulun'" (Judges 4:6). God and Deborah had a plan: to draw Jabin's general, Sisera, out to meet the challenge of Barak and his men. But Barak didn't immediately get on board with this daring stratagem.

Barak said to her, "If you will go with me, I will go; but if you will not go with me, I will not go." (Judges 4:8)

Like any informed Israelite, Barak knew they were badly outgunned, and it doesn't appear he was excited about taking on Sisera and his vast array of military armaments. How many times have we reacted like he did? *Lord, I know you're telling me to do X, but I'm really ill-equipped. You can't mean that, can you?*

Not so for Deborah. She *knew* she'd heard from God directly, and she was just delivering the message. She had total confidence in what He had instructed her to do.

> And she said, "I will surely go with you; nevertheless, the road on which you are going will not lead to your glory, for the Lord will sell Sisera into the hand of a woman." (Judges 4:9)

Boy, is that an interesting twist in the story! Not only is Deborah a bold and brave leader, but she prophecies that yet another woman will take down Sisera: Jael. (We'll meet Jael in the pages ahead.) Barak's reluctance cost him a piece of the victory.

Despite his hesitation, Barak rallied ten thousand men from the tribes of Naphtali and Zebulun, and along with Deborah, they headed to the battlefield. I've often wondered what Sisera thought of these underdogs. Did he view them as foolish to attempt to confront his massive, well-equipped army?

Once Sisera had them in place, Deborah confidently proclaimed:

> "Go! This is the day the Lord has given Sisera into your hands. Has not the Lord gone ahead of you?" (Judges 4:14)

And with that, Barak and his men headed into the fray full steam ahead!

> And the Lord routed Sisera and all his chariots and all his army before Barak at the end of the sword; and Sisera alighted from his chariot and fled away on foot. And

> Barak pursued the chariots and the army to Harosheth-ha-goyim, and all the army of Sisera fell by the sword; not a man was left. (Judges 4:15–16)

This one wasn't even close. It wasn't as if Israel squeaked out a victory and called it a day. No, Barak and his army of hill people (on foot no less) defeated an army equipped with hundreds of chariots and warhorses. The Bible says not a single man from the army under Sisera's command was left, except for their hapless commander! This was nothing short of an act of God, a miracle. Sisera abandoned his treasured iron chariot and was forced to flee on foot. (We'll catch up with him in a bit.)

What we see in the following chapter, Judges 5, is a work of art. Not only was Deborah a prophetess and judge who had just overseen the miraculous overthrow of an enemy oppressing her people, but she was also credited with creating a victory song that is one of the longest poetic compositions in all of the Bible. Deborah and Barak joined in a song that has echoes of Moses and the people of Israel by the Red Sea. The Song of Deborah tells the history of Israel's wars and the power of God fighting for His people.

The constant refrain of this victory song is "Bless the Lord!" and it's worth pausing for a minute to consider this phrase, which is one we hear again and again in the pages of Scripture. What exactly does it mean? What is the listener being asked to do when we say, "Bless the Lord"? It's the same phrase that Jesus used when he taught us to pray "hallowed be Thy Name." We are being asked to help make God's name holy with our words as well as our deeds. We bless the Lord when we praise Him and also when we serve Him. Deborah's call to her people was a call to surrender themselves to their God in thought and deed and in word and action.

The Song of Deborah was also aimed outward, at the kings and people surrounding them. Israel never forgot that the drama of their relationship with God was happening in full view of other nations and as a witness to them. Deborah emphasized this at the beginning of her song:

Hear, O kings; give ear, O princes
To the Lord I will sing
I will make melody to the Lord, the God of Israel. (Judges 5:3)

There is an evangelistic core at the heart of the Song of Deborah. Of course, Deborah wanted to strengthen and encourage her people's faith by reminding them of the miracle God had just worked for them. But she also hadn't forgotten that what happened to Israel happened in view of the whole world. Deborah hoped that her song would he heard by "you who sit on rich carpets" and "to the sound of musicians at the watering places." There she hoped that they would "repeat the triumphs of the Lord, the triumphs of his peasantry in Israel" (Judges 5:10-11). That quaint word, *peasantry*, is one she repeats a couple of times in the song. It's a way of contrasting Israel's relative poverty with the wealth and power of the nations around it. The people of Israel were basically farmers, without the kind of trade resources their neighbors (or Jabin) had at their disposal. But God intervened for them anyway, reaching down into their lives to work a miracle that would give them their freedom back, something He did time and time again.

Deborah sings of just how bad the conditions were for her

people, how demoralized they were before defeating Sisera and his army.

> . . . the highways were abandoned
> travelers took to winding paths.
> Villagers in Israel would not fight;
> they held back until I, Deborah, arose,
> until I arose, a mother in Israel.
> God chose new leaders
> when war came to the city gates,
> but not a shield or spear was seen
> among forty thousand in Israel. (Judges 5:6–8)

It sure sounds like people had just given up. Their highways were so unsafe that they wouldn't use them. And in contrast to the sweet gear Sisera had, "not a shield or spear was seen among forty thousand in Israel." These people were down for the count.

As befits a woman of action, most of the Song of Deborah is taken up with describing the course of the battle. Deborah praised not only the tribes of Zebulun and Naphtali who fought with their kinsman Barak, but also the tribes who volunteered to help remove Jabin's yoke, Benjamin and Issachar especially. She also heaped scorn on the tribes that chose to skip the battle: Reuben and Dan and Asher, the last of whom "remained on the coast and stayed in his coves" (Judges 5:17).

Did these tribes consider Deborah and Barak's plans and think, *I don't like those odds. I think I'll sit this one out*? From a practical and political standpoint, their decision likely made sense. After all, there was little guarantee that Barak and Deborah's plan would work. Some scattered tribesmen on foot against a trained professional army with hundreds of chariots and warhorses? Come on. And if the Israelites did fail, Jabin and Sisera's wrath would be scorching. Why stir the hornets' nest? There have always been and always will be people who don't want to rock the boat any-time God tells His people, "Go!" Judges 5:16 tells us that "in the districts of Reuben there was much searching of heart." This sug-gests that there were others who could have gotten involved in the effort, but who spent too much time hemming and hawing about it. Deborah wasn't going to let them off the hook so easily. Instead, she publicly called them out in her song of triumph.

When we get to the battle scene, Deborah's poetry reaches a powerful crescendo:

> From heaven fought the stars,
> From their course they fought against Sisera.
> The torrent Kishon swept them away,
> the onrushing torrent, the torrent Kishon.
> March on, my soul, with might!
> Then loud beat the horses' hoofs
> with the galloping, galloping of his steeds. (Judges 5:21–22)

Notice what an extraordinary thing Deborah says here. At the beginning of the song, she speaks to the surrounding kings and peoples. She also seems to personify the stars as the source of the floodwaters that bogged down those fancy chariots. Some schol-ars believe the reference is a swipe at the Canaanites' belief in astrology, with Deborah saying, "So much for the stars backing you up!" To her, Israel was never some forgotten corner of the universe filled with insignificant hill farmers. She knew that, in God's eyes, His people and their survival were a priority.

Too often we hesitate like those tribes of Dan and Asher and Reuben, refusing to believe God's miraculous promises. In fear, rather than confidence, we refuse to take the risk of trusting God, to take Him at His unfailing word. What if we could summon the courage of Deborah, whose heart was obviously so closely aligned with God's that she didn't doubt His direction in a situation that, by human standards, appeared to be a death sentence?

The Song of Deborah closes with a powerful image. It ends with the picture of Sisera's mother anxiously waiting for her son to arrive home:

Out of the window she peered,
The mother of Sisera gazed through the lattice:
"Why is his chariot so long in coming?
Why tarry the hoofbeats of his chariot?"
Her wisest ladies make no answer
Nay, she gives answer to herself,
"Are they not finding and dividing the spoil?
A maiden or two for every man; spoil of dyed stuffs for Sisera." (Judges 5:28–30)

That is some hard reading. It's difficult to internalize the image of a woman sitting waiting for her son to come home from war, especially when we as readers know how Sisera's story ends. But we have to look at the reality of what was going on here. The language Deborah uses suggests that Sisera's mother was implying that her son was out not simply having a good time, but more specifically, sexually assaulting young women. The passage implies that the values of this woman, mother or not, were ultimately pagan.

We see motherhood woven throughout the Song of Deborah, first in Deborah describing herself as a mother who arose in Israel when it seemed everyone else had given up (Judges 5:7). Most of the images of motherhood in the Bible are ones of nurturing, of tenderness and protectiveness and caring. The people of Israel in the Bible are nomadic and agricultural, simple people living close to the land. Their ideas of women's and men's roles are equally simple: men fought the wars, and women took care of the children. But in Deborah's story, we see that motherhood can also be something fierce and warlike. Deborah was chosen and equipped by God, full of discernment and bravery at a time when the people of Israel needed rescuing, both spiritually and physically.

But by revisiting motherhood in her song—this time via the story of a mother who would soon be grieving—Deborah makes another important point. She offers a very human illustration of the realities of war, and I think we can infer she was sending a message.

"So may all your enemies perish, Lord!
But may all who love you be like the sun
when it rises in its strength." (Judges 5:31)

As Deborah and Barak led the Israelites in celebrating a miraculous conquest, they also put the rest of their enemies on notice: *Hey, see what happens when the people of Israel, backed by their unbeatable God, show up for battle?*

Deborah's joyous celebration ends with this final line: "Then the land had peace forty years" (Judges 5:31). What an about-face from the moments when her story started. When we first meet her, Israel is in big trouble. True, it earned it. The people had done "evil in the eyes of the Lord" (Judges 4:1). They were being terrorized by their enemies, cruelly oppressed for twenty years, and they begged the Lord for help. He sent them Deborah, who led them to peace.

I find so much encouragement and direction in her story. It's no fluke that God chose and prepared this woman. He gave her gifts of discernment and understanding that caused her to be revered and trusted by her people. They came to her with their disputes. How many times have you been caught in that place—bickering children, disgruntled coworkers, gossiping friends? We don't have to be leading a nation to face some of the responsibilities Deborah faced. But there's something we can do. We can take a breath, listen to a frustrated friend, seek God's truth, and try to lovingly bring peace to all the frustrations we encounter in our daily lives.

Deborah spoke truth with confidence. She didn't try to minimize the reality of the situation, but she did choose to believe in God's faithfulness. How many of us hesitate to speak up when God has asked us to, directed us to? Do we worry about how the words will be received, that people will think we've overstepped boundaries or lost touch with reality? Deborah didn't! She had a message directly from God, and she simply delivered it. It wasn't up to her, and it's not up to us, to water down God's perfect plans. We are simply called to follow His lead and leave the rest up to Him.

Where can you and I be more like Deborah in our own lives, stepping out in faith and trusting God for the victory? Deborah wasn't tasked with poring over battle plans with Barak and figuring out every detail before showing up how, when, and where God told her to. Most of the time, we won't get a perfect road map for our spiritual journeys, either. But as one of my favorite verses promises, God is "able to do immeasurably more than all we ask or imagine, according to his power that is at work within us" (Ephesians 3:20).

Now, about Sisera . . .

JAEL
(Judges 4:17–23, 5:24–27)

The story of Jael is a wild one, complete with betrayal and murder and more than a few unanswered questions. Let's start here: she was a killer.

Her story at first strikes the reader as rather short and sweet, but it goes much deeper. Jael not only fulfilled one of Deborah's prophecies, but she also killed a man who had "cruelly" oppressed the Israelites for twenty years. Her actions capped off an unexpected, momentous victory by Israel that launched its people into a new era of peace. So, let's take a look.

After the slaughter of Sisera's army led by Deborah and Barak, Sisera took off in search of an escape to safety. In his panic, he found a place that must have seemed like the perfect hideaway.

Sisera, meanwhile, fled on foot to the tent of Jael, the wife of Heber the Kenite, because there was an alliance between Jabin king of Hazor and the family of Heber the Kenite. (Judges 4:17)

The Kenite people were nomadic, living in tents, often in areas close to the tribes of Israel. They were the people of Jethro, Moses's father-in-law, and so they had a kind of cousinhood with the people of Israel. But Jethro's people remained independent, even though they were often closely allied with the people of Israel and settled near them. Their stories often intertwined. In 1 Samuel 15:6, we see King Saul praise and thank the Kenites, "for you showed kindness to all the Israelites when they came up out of Egypt." Whatever that graciousness had been, by the time we meet Heber the Kenite in Judges, he's allied with a king who is tormenting and mistreating the people of Israel. For that reason, Sisera must have felt a sense of protection or refuge in Jael's tent. Remember, Jael was not Jewish. She was not one of the children of Israel. Like Ruth and Rahab (whom we'll meet later), she was a Gentile, an outsider.

Confident in his alliance with this woman, Sisera, likely emotionally and physically exhausted from battle, was desperate for refuge.

> And Jael came out to meet Sisera, and said to him, "Turn aside, my lord, turn aside to me; have no fear." So he turned aside to her into the tent, and she covered him with a rug. And he said to her, "Pray, give me a little water to drink; for I am thirsty." So she opened a skin of milk and gave him a drink and covered him. And he said to her, "Stand at the door of the tent, and if any man comes and asks you, 'Is anyone here,' say, No." (Judges 4:17–20)

Hospitality was the law of the land, and Jael played the part to perfection. She treated her guest with deference, getting him a drink and making him comfortable . . . but not for long. After Sisera specifically instructed her to hide him and to deny that he was there, she leapt into action.

> But Jael, Heber's wife, picked up a tent peg and a hammer and went quietly to him while he lay fast asleep, exhausted. She drove the peg through his temple into the ground, and he died. (Judges 4:21)

Open-and-shut case, we can imagine the prosecutor saying. Let's just look at all the laws Jael has violated here: the law of hospitality, which says that a guest must never be harmed; the law of submission, which says that a woman must serve a man; the law of God, which says that murder of a defenseless individual is a sacrilege. *But, wait!* says the defense. *That's not the whole story.* Jael's actions stemmed directly from the obedience and bravery of Deborah. Let's not forget, Barak gave up his position of "honor" or "glory" because he didn't immediately heed the words of God sent to him through Deborah, and because of that, she prophesied that "the Lord will deliver Sisera into the hands of a woman" (Judges 4:9). He most certainly did!

As is sometimes the case with its characters, the Bible doesn't tell us what is happening in Jael's head as this prophecy is being fulfilled. It seems that whatever Heber's decisions and alliances were, Jael saw things differently the moment Sisera showed up at her home. We know nothing of what Jael's life was like before this, but it seems she must have felt some level of sympathy for the people of Israel. Had she seen the brutal treatment they'd suffered at the hands of Jabin and Sisera? Was she simply moved by the Spirit of God to rescue His people after they cried out to Him? After all, He had provided Deborah, and they bravely followed her leadership into battle.

Though we can't know her motives for certain, her actions leave no doubt. Notice that she didn't even wait for Sisera to come to her; she went out to meet him. Was Jael already formulating a plan in her head before Sisera even said a word? She encouraged him to turn aside to her tent and to "have no fear." We know, with hindsight, that Sisera had a lot to fear, but Jael worked hard to put him at ease and to make sure he relaxed. She covered him with a blanket, and when he asked for water, she did him one better and gave him milk—much like a mother hoping to calm a child and make him drowsy. She did everything possible to make him think he was safe, and honored, and treated as he would have been in his own palace. And then she struck! By the way, the name "Jael" means "mountain goat." Think of the comparison: a gutsy woman who produced milk and proved to be pretty tough!

> Just then Barak came by in pursuit of Sisera, and Jael went out to meet him. "Come," she said, "I will show you the man you're looking for." So he went in with her, and there lay Sisera with the tent peg through his temple—dead. (Judges 4:22)

I can see this playing out like a scene in a movie. The whole area is transfixed by a bloody battle that has claimed the lives of thousands. A mighty army with the best military equipment around has just been upended, with not a single soldier left alive. Its top general has just ducked into the tent of a stranger, no doubt reeling from the enormous, stunning loss. His hostess kills him. Just then, the general from the other side sprints up in hot pursuit of the first general, only to be calmly informed by the woman, *I've got your man, and he's dead.* She didn't try to hide it. No, she bravely approached Israel's top commander and exposed what she'd done.

What kinds of consequences would Jael, the wife of Heber, have stood to face? Surely, she knew that after she assassinated Sisera, her husband's alliance with Jabin would be over. Would her marriage be done, too? After all, what Jael did was in direct conflict with the agreement or understanding Heber had reached with Jabin. In killing Sisera, Jael put everything on the line. Would her husband throw her out, refuse to speak to her again, refuse to give her even so much as a skin of water to carry with her into the desert? It was not a small thing that Jael was risking in order to throw in her lot with the people of Israel; it was her whole life.

And here's the thing about Jael: she did have a choice. If Esther, for instance (whom we'll meet later), had walked away from her people's plight, she would have been guilty of abandoning them in their hour of need. Mordecai knew it and warned her that even she, as queen, would not be safe. He also admonished her that if she did not rise up to save the Jews, someone else would. He knew Esther was in the palace "for such a time as this" (Esther 4:14). Esther didn't act in a vacuum, but Jael could have. What if she had simply decided to give Sisera some water and a place to rest? No one would have condemned her. But like Rahab, Jael made a choice that benefited not her own people, but the people of Israel. She could have stayed quiet and carried on with her life, but she saw the people of Israel in need, and she responded.

Jael picked up a tent peg and drove it through the skull of a sleeping Sisera. If she had been discovered at any point, she would have been killed instantly. Picture her quietly creeping through the tent, getting closer and closer to the sleeping Sisera. The Bible tells us that she moved "softly," and in that one word, we can see how slowly and carefully and with what bated breath she must have moved. What if Sisera had awakened while the tent peg was against his temple—what then? Even though it represents just a few short words in the Bible, there were so many points at which Jael's plan could have gone wrong. No matter what she felt inside, Jael would have worked to stay calm and to summon all the strength she had.

Finally, we get to the idea of the tent peg itself. Why would she have chosen this as the murder weapon? In nomadic cultures, women were the ones responsible for setting up and removing the tents. They were the ones who decided not only how to manage and arrange the household within the tent, but where the tent should go and how to set it up. Women quite literally built the home. So, for Jael to have had a tent peg and hammer at hand, and to have known how to use it, would not have been unusual. These items would have represented domesticity, hospitality, and safety—how a home came together, not how it turned into a crime scene. Jael took these deeply symbolic tools and used them to end the life of a general fleeing a devastating battle, one that launched the Israelites on a path to resounding victory.

Right after she tells Barak what she's done, we read:

On that day God subdued Jabin king of Canaan before the Israelites. And the hand of the Israelites pressed harder and harder against Jabin king of Canaan until they destroyed him. (Judges 4:23-24)

A chapter that begins with the blunt statement "Again, the Israelites did evil in the sight of the Lord" ends with the resounding defeat of a king who caused them so much pain—with two women, Deborah and Jael, playing the starring roles.

So, what do we make of the idea of a woman warrior? Well, here is what the Song of Deborah has to say about Jael:

> Most blessed of women be Jael,
> the wife of Heber the Kenite,
> of tent-dwelling women most blessed.
> He asked water and she gave him milk,
> she brought him curds in a lordly bowl.
> She put her hand to the tent peg
> and her right hand to the workmen's mallet;
> she struck Sisera a blow,
> she crushed his head,
> she shattered and pierced his temple. (Judges 5:24-26)

"Most blessed of women" is quite a vaunted position! In the Song of Deborah, Jael is given a hero's treatment. She was the one who took decisive action when God put her in a place to act. She was proactive, in contrast to Barak's initial reluctance. One of the most extraordinary things about the Song of Deborah is that it is one of the few instances in the Bible where one woman praises another in this way. It is also an instance where a woman is the subject of a prophecy. Just as God had prepared and established Deborah to right His people and lead them to victory, Jael was positioned exactly where God needed her to be to give His people the upper hand and a final victory over Jabin.

In the battles He sets before us, God expects us to fight as Jael did, with the weapons we have. And He gives us plenty of them, weapons much stronger than the nine hundred chariots of iron that didn't save Sisera and his men. As we'll learn in our New Testament study, God first sent His Son and then the Holy Spirit, God, with us and in us to equip us. He's also given us some very practical encouragement and armor, as Paul outlines in Ephesians:

Finally, be strong in the Lord and in his mighty power. Put on the full armor of God, so that you can take your stand against the devil's schemes. For our struggle is not against flesh and blood, but against the rulers, against the authorities, against the powers of this dark world and against the spiritual forces of evil in the heavenly realms. Therefore put on the full armor of God, so that when the day of evil comes, you may be able to stand your ground, and after you have done everything, to stand. Stand firm then, with the belt of truth buckled around your waist, with the breastplate of righteousness in place, and with your feet fitted with the readiness that comes from the gospel of peace. In addition to all this, take up the shield of faith, with which you can extinguish all the flaming arrows of the evil one. Take the helmet of salvation and the sword of the Spirit, which is the word of God. (Ephesians 6:10–17)

Sisera isn't going to show up at our homes, but the enemy is—count on that. No, we won't be picking up a tent peg, but we absolutely must arm ourselves with truth, righteousness, peace, faith, and more. Most of us will never live anywhere near an earthly battlefield like Deborah or Jael, but we're living on a spiritual one every day.

Paul goes on to talk about the power of prayer, and it may be the mightiest of weapons we possess today. He admonishes believers:

And pray in the Spirit on all occasions with all kinds of prayers and requests. With this in mind, be alert and always keep on praying for all the Lord's people. (Ephesians 6:18)

We can wrap ourselves, our families, our loved ones, and our leaders in the protection of prayer—and we're called to do so! It's a theme Paul revisits in 2 Corinthians 10:

> For though we live in the world, we do not wage war as the world does. The weapons we fight with are not the weapons of the world. On the contrary, they have divine power to demolish strongholds. We demolish arguments and every pretension that sets itself up against the knowledge of God, and we take captive every thought to make it obedient to Christ.

In a very real sense, we are called to be modern-day warriors in the mold of Deborah and Jael. They didn't model timidity and hesitation for us. Instead, they gave us an example of obedience and action.

Scripture doesn't tell us whether Deborah and Jael ever met, but I've often wondered. Jael took Barak straight to Sisera's lifeless body. Did he then urge her to run back to Deborah with him, to testify to what she'd done? He must have recognized Jael as the very fulfillment of Deborah's prophecy.

How must Jael have felt to have an A-list position in the victory party, to be honored in the exultant song of praise that Deborah and Barak proclaimed, to hear herself called most blessed of women? The beauty of the Jael story is the way it turns so many expectations on their head. Jael was expected to offer hospitality to Sisera, and she offered him the opposite. Her husband was aligned with Israel's enemy, and yet here she was being lauded and applauded by her husband's enemies. Israel had an incredible reversal of fortune that day because of God's favor, as two women changed the course of history by being God's one-two punch, His prophetess and His warrior.

Whatever battle you may have been through, or are fighting now, or will one day face, God will be with you. He is faithful to equip and guide you. He provides us with a vast array of weapons, but it is up to us to be prepared and willing. How much effort am I spending saturating my mind and my heart with truth? How much Scripture is tucked into my memory banks so that when the enemy shows up, I can shut him down with God's powerful words? And how much time am I spending in prayer, seeking His will and praying His powerful promises over my own home and those I love? Like Deborah and Jael, I want to be armed and ready when my assignment arrives!

Deborah and Jael Study Questions

1. Jael and her husband were Kenites, a tribe with ancient connections to the people of Israel. Moses's father-in-law, Jethro, and wife, Zipporah, were Kenites, so intermarriage between Jews and Kenites was not seen as the same sort of threat to Israel's religion that intermarriage between Jews and Canaanites was. Take a look at the following passages to trace the history of the Kenites and discuss what that can tell us of their relationship to Israel: Genesis 15:18–21, Exodus 3:1, Numbers 10:29, Judges 1:16 and 4:11, and 1 Samuel 15:6. What does this mean for how we see Jael?

2. Although Jael's story is an example of a woman's violence against a man, most often in Bible stories, the violence runs in the other direction. In both Genesis 19 (the story of Lot) and Judges 19 (the story of the Levite's concubine), women are offered up to violent mobs. Read those stories, then think about what separates Jael's violent action from those violent actions. What does the Bible tell us about the difference between the vulnerable and the powerful?

3. Deborah assumes leadership at a troubled time for Israel. Looking at the "before" and "after" can tell us things about Deborah, too. The judges Ehud and Shamgar preceded her, and Ehud also killed a leader of Israel's enemy in order to bring about victory. Look at Judges 3:7–30. How was Ehud's action different from Deborah's? Why does God play a prominent part in Deborah's story but is absent in Ehud's? The Bible tells us that with Deborah as judge, "the

land had peace forty years" (Judges 5:31). What happened after that forty-year period? Read Judges 6:1–10. What did the people of Israel do, and what did the prophet tell them?

4. The next judge to arise was the famous hero Gideon. Read Judges 6: 11–16. What is Gideon's complaint against God? Does God answer his question? In what way?

Speaking God's Truth

HANNAH
(1 Samuel 1:1–2:21)

First Samuel begins the narrative that will weave through so much of the Old Testament: the story of David. King David's life and journey, which covers three books of the Bible and the Psalms, begins with Abraham and ends with a shepherd boy from the hill country eventually becoming king and uniting all the tribes of Israel. But in order to have David, we have to have Samuel, the prophet who anointed David to his great calling. And to have Samuel, we have to have Hannah. So, Hannah stands right at the center of this unfolding story. Once again, a woman is included in the pages of the Bible not only as a central character in the dramatic adventure that leads us to the arrival of our Savior, but also to teach us important lessons about faithfulness and redemption in the midst of pain.

As we saw in the stories of Sarah and Rachel, Hannah ached for a child of her own. In the pages of the Old Testament, we see the longing and despair of infertility in a culture that saw the blessing of children as the greatest possible good and a sign of God's favor. To be denied motherhood in that time must have felt like being shut out of God's grace. And it was especially painful to be compared to other women who not only had children of their own, but also turned that beautiful gift into a weapon by mocking and belittling the childless. That's right where we meet our heroine, Hannah.

So, who was she? Hannah was not the wife of a powerful chieftain like Abraham or Jacob. She was married to a common man from an obscure village in the hill country of Ephraim. About her husband, Elkanah, we know only that he was financially secure enough to support two wives—which may not have meant that he was all that prosperous. He was a Levite by birth, but he was living in a non-Levitical town. Yet Scripture tells us that, every year, he went up from his town of Ramathaim to Shiloh, to present a sacrifice to God. And from that sacrifice, the priests would return to him meat to be eaten by him and his family, a ritual portion of food. It's here that we first see just how devoted Elkanah is to Hannah in her childless sorrow:

> Whenever the day came for Elkanah to sacrifice, he would give portions of the meat to his wife Peninnah and to all her sons and daughters. But to Hannah he gave a double portion because he loved her, and the Lord had closed her womb. (1 Samuel 1:4–5)

Elkanah didn't give Hannah what custom dictated. Instead, he gave her double, signaling his love and care for her despite her lack of children.

I think for most women, it's easy to connect with Hannah,

whether you've dealt with infertility or not. We all know what it's like to worry that a deep desire may go unfulfilled. What's worse is to have people know of that unmet longing and for them to leverage that ache into additional pain by taunting us and our open wounds. That's exactly what Hannah was facing. Peninnah wasn't satisfied to find contentment in her own full life; she had to rub Hannah's face in it, hit her where her heart ached most:

> Because the Lord had closed Hannah's womb, her rival kept provoking her in order to irritate her. This went on year after year. Whenever Hannah went up to the house of the Lord, her rival provoked her till she wept and would not eat. (1 Samuel 1:6–7)

Let's sit with that for just a minute. It's difficult enough to imagine sharing our spouse with anyone else, let alone longing for a child who won't materialize. But the final blow came from Elkanah's other wife: not only did she have many children of her own, but she jeered at and insulted Hannah to the point of weeping and complete despair over her barrenness. Hannah wasn't grieving with the support of another woman who walked alongside her in her anguish. Instead, she must have felt isolated and attacked. Rather than sharing the burden, Peninnah was adding to it, in a big way.

Elkanah might have been married to two women, but it was Hannah he loved—much like Jacob loved Rachel. Like Rachel, Hannah was the chosen spouse, but she was also the childless one. The joy of being loved was counterbalanced against the misery of missing out on motherhood. Elkanah could see that Hannah was suffering:

Her husband Elkanah would say to her, "Hannah, why are you weeping? Why don't you eat? Why are you down-hearted? Don't I mean more to you than ten sons?" (1 Samuel 1:8)

To me, Elkanah's words seem to indicate that their marriage was about much more than just producing heirs and descendants. If anything, Elkanah felt that his deep love for Hannah was more than enough. She wasn't around just to expand his family; he adored her. And yet, I often wonder if he was privy to the abuse she was receiving at Peninnah's hands. Were the insults and jeers leveled beyond his earshot? Hannah's tears weren't only about being barren. They were also about the stinging salt constantly being thrown onto her wound.

Scripture doesn't tell us what Hannah's response was, if any. But we do know she took action: she stood up from the table and went to pray at the tabernacle. One of the most comforting things about our God is that He is always there awaiting our prayers, even when we can't find the words to express our deepest grief. Sometimes our hurts are so delicate and raw that we don't have the strength to share that level of vulnerability with another human being. God already knows the deepest recesses of our heart, so going to Him only ushers us into the safest of all possible places we can be. Philippians 4 counsels us not to be anxious about anything, "but in every situation, by prayer and petition, with thanksgiving, present your requests to God" (Philippians 4:6). And that's exactly what Hannah did:

In her deep anguish Hannah prayed to the Lord, weeping bitterly. And she made a vow, saying, "Lord Almighty, if you will only look on your servant's misery and remember me, and not forget your servant but give her a son, then I will give him to the Lord for all the days of his life, and no razor will ever be used on his head." (1 Samuel 1:10-11)

Hannah called out to the Lord—*remember me, see my misery, please don't forget me.* Whatever your struggle, this prayer works. The next verse tells us that even after she made this promise to God to give up her firstborn son, "she kept on praying to the Lord" (1 Samuel 1:12). She didn't put her offer on the table and walk away. No, she continued to pour out her heart to God.

It's not that Hannah said, *Okay, if you give me this thing I really want, I will give you this other thing.* She didn't try to strike a bargain with God. Making an offering to God isn't about God, but about us. It's not that God needs anything from us. Making an offering to God is about making sure that just as in any loving relationship, we are not simply taking from our beloved, but also giving in return.

As Hannah was making her pledge, her story took an interesting turn. You see, Eli the priest had been watching Hannah "weeping bitterly" and he jumped to an incorrect conclusion.

Hannah was praying in her heart, and her lips were moving, but her voice was not being heard. Eli thought she was drunk and said to her, "How long are you going to stay drunk? Put away your wine."

Ouch! Have you ever been stung by someone getting the wrong first impression of you at your weakest, most desperate moment? We've all been the victim, and we've probably all been the perpetrator, too. This moment always makes me wince and think about when I've been guilty of misjudging someone or their circumstances, and this was a woman who needed some comforting!

So, a little bit of historical context feels necessary here. Two things the ancient world found very strange were silent praying and silent reading. In each case, you'd expect to hear someone's voice. Today it's commonplace for someone to close their eyes and pray silently, but that was not the normal method of prayer in the times when Eli served as a priest, so he made a faulty assumption. Hannah, in what was undoubtedly one of her most vulnerable moments, explains:

> "Not so, my lord," Hannah replied, "I am a woman who is deeply troubled. I have not been drinking wine or beer; I was pouring out my soul to the Lord. Do not take your servant for a wicked woman; I have been praying here out of my great anguish and grief." (1 Samuel 1:15–16)

Please don't get the wrong impression of me, sir! I'm throwing myself before God and begging Him for help.

We see no indication that Hannah ever told Eli *why* she was so troubled, only that she was, but he quickly saw her heart and her need. He told her to go in peace, adding, "[M]ay the God of Israel grant you what you have asked of him" (1 Samuel 1:17). Those words of reassurance were just what she needed. The Bible tells us she went on her way, finally ate something, "and her face was no longer downcast" (1 Samuel 1:18). There is so much power in the words of encouragement we share with others, loved ones or strangers. The scene with Hannah and Eli reminds me of Proverbs 16:24:

Gracious words are a honeycomb,
sweet to the soul and healing to the bones.

Isn't this just what Hannah needed, some sweetness and healing? Eli could have added to her grief, and he certainly started
down that path, but he quickly turned the situation around, sharing words that gave her what she needed most in her anguish:
hope. Let this be a lesson for us, to step in and lift up those around
us who are suffering.

Not long after Hannah and Elkanah returned home, she became pregnant and had a son. What overwhelming joy she must
have felt! Her years of crying out to God were not in vain. Her
willingness to pray and weep openly and humbly at the tabernacle, asking for His help, bore fruit at last. She named her firstborn "Samuel"—"Shemu-el," in the Hebrew, for "God had heard."
Hannah was given her little boy. During the time she nursed
and raised him, she did not go with the rest of the family on the
yearly pilgrimage to Shiloh. But once he had reached the traditional age of weaning, she packed up her most precious gift and
took him back to Shiloh, where she had so fervently prayed that
he would one day arrive. It was time for her to reintroduce herself to Eli the priest.

And she said to him, "Pardon me, my lord. As surely as
you live, I am the woman who stood here beside you praying to the Lord. I prayed for this child, and the Lord has
granted me what I asked of him. So now I give him to the
Lord. For his whole life he will be given over to the Lord."
(1 Samuel 1:26–28)

Nowhere in Scripture do we see a moment of hesitation from Hannah. She had promised God that if He sent her a son, she would return that young boy in service to Him. It's hard for us to wrap our human minds around the idea of dropping off a little boy, probably about the age of three, to live hours (maybe days) away with people he's never met. But it appears Hannah was at total peace with fulfilling the promise she'd made.

In reading Hannah's story, we can't help but think back to Abraham's story and his decision to follow God's command and offer Isaac in sacrifice. In each case, the parent was faced with giving up their beloved child, a foreshadowing of what God Himself did in sending us Jesus. No matter what emotions or human objections may surface in our own minds as we follow along in Scripture, in each case, we see steady obedience to God's call. Is there anything in our lives we're clinging to too tightly? Are we refusing to let God have control of a situation or cherishing the gifts we've been given over the giver Himself? We wouldn't be human if we didn't sometimes try to rationalize these things.

It's a daily process, at least for me, of choosing to lay down what I've become too attached to. I like to think of myself as someone who's been through enough valleys to have earned a measure of maturity, but reality often puts a mirror up to my face, and I don't always like what I see. When the COVID-19 pandemic hit, I realized I was really rattled. People were getting very ill and dying. Domestically and around the world, economies and markets were shaken, and so many of the comforts of life—hugging a friend or sharing a meal at a restaurant—were suddenly out of the question. It was a jolt. And it was a reset for me. It quickly became painfully obvious to me just how many *things* were bringing me comfort and ease, when instead, I should have been fully grounded and rooted in my Heavenly Father. I asked myself what I was willing to part with in order to find complete and unchanging joy in God. Following Hannah's example, I put the things I cherished most into God's hands and into His service.

For Hannah, it was a joyful decision. The very next thing we hear from her is a song of praise, among the most magnificent poetry in the Bible. The Song of Hannah is the longest prayer of its kind in the Old Testament, and it became a model of sorts for other prayers we see later in Scripture:

"My heart rejoices in the Lord; in the Lord my horn is lifted high. My mouth boasts over my enemies, for I delight in your deliverance. There is no one holy like the Lord; there is no one besides you; there is no Rock like our God." (1 Samuel 2:1–2)

In my mind's eye, I imagine Hannah with her hands lifted high to heaven, maybe even dancing as she pours out her heart. With that remarkable statement as its jumping-off point, where did Hannah's prayer go next? Her clear vision was of a God of absolute power who could alter any condition in life at His will:

"The Lord brings death and makes alive; he brings down to the grave and raises up. The Lord sends poverty and wealth; he humbles and he exalts. He raises the poor from the dust and lifts the needy from the ash heap; he seats them with princes and has them inherit a throne of honor." (1 Samuel 2:6–8)

Hannah's God is the God of reversal. He upended death. He alone could humble and exalt. He took people who had nothing and gave them everything. She had lived this reality, and her view of God's infinite power was broader than her own little hill village of Ramathaim. Hannah also put a spotlight on a truth we see again and again in Scripture: that God's ways are not the ways of the world.

> "It is not by strength that one prevails;
> those who oppose the Lord will be broken.
> The Most High will thunder from heaven;
> the Lord will judge the ends of the earth." (1 Samuel 2:9b–10a)

As we see throughout His Word, God confounds the world by working through people who aren't the strongest or most gifted. It's the contrast between our human frailty and His boundless power that winds up directing the glory where it belongs: to Him.

I love that we get some more insight into how Hannah's life continued as Samuel grew in his service to God. She and Elkanah continued in their faithful sacrifices and to see their young son, and "each year his mother made him a little robe and took it to him" (1 Samuel 2:19). What a precious detail to include in this story. How she must have loved working on that project every year, looking forward to giving the new garment to Samuel in person. Their family visits also brought new encouragement each year:

> Eli would bless Elkanah and his wife, saying, "May the Lord give you children by this woman to take the place

of the one she prayed for and gave to the Lord." Then they would go home. (1 Samuel 2:20).

God was good. Hannah had three sons and two daughters. A woman who spent years in misery and despair, taunted by her unkind rival, became a mother to many. Such joy! It's impossible to out-give God. As Christ spells out in the Gospel of Luke:

Give, and it will be given to you. A good measure, pressed down, shaken together and running over, will be poured into your lap. For with the measure you use, it will be measured to you. (Luke 6:38)

In addition to raising her growing brood at home, Hannah was also able to watch Samuel grow into a great prophet, one who served God and who would one day anoint King David to lead His people. It was in guiding Samuel to David that we see God reveal one of His greatest truths:

The Lord does not look at the things people look at. People look at the outward appearance, but the Lord looks at the heart. (1 Samuel 16:7b)

How true this rings for Hannah. He saw her grief and longing, even as Eli initially misjudged her. God saw her years of heartache, the cruel insults from Peninnah. He also saw in her a faithful woman who would birth a prophet to guide His people.

The words of Hannah's prayer echoed down through the centuries. They soaked into the souls of devout Jews. And when, hundreds of years later, another devout Jewish woman who also experienced God reaching into her life was searching for words to express that miracle, she may have turned to Hannah's words as a model. The Song of Mary (which we'll read in the pages ahead) and the Song of Hannah express the same truth: a God who works in unexpected ways, who changes circumstances in radical fashion and who uses the humble and unknown to carry out His greatest plans. Both Mary and Hannah saw beyond the limited vision of events happening in their own lives to comprehend the much bigger picture.

Hannah is an exquisite example of faith. As she endured years of longing and harassment, she didn't allow Peninnah's taunting to make her bitter. Was she wounded? Yes. But we never see that she returned the venom or plotted against the woman who caused her so much pain. Instead, she allowed her agony to drive her straight to the only source who could help her. God knew every delicate, hurtful circumstance of her life, every detail. She took Him all her baggage and asked for His mercy. She continued in faithful prayer, prayer so passionate that it drew attention at the tabernacle. Hannah went boldly and openly to God with her request.

Is there some wound or need so deep in your life that, like Hannah, you should lay it at God's feet? Is there a relationship that seems beyond repair, a financial hole, a dream that seems will never become a reality? There's nothing stopping you but your own hesitation. We don't have to travel to a tabernacle or temple. If we've placed our trust in Him, God is in us and with us every minute of every hour of every single day, without fail. Just think, Hannah's decision to lay it all on the line set the foundation for the nation of Israel to one day be united under King

David, identified as a man after God's own heart. One woman had the faith to turn aside from her critics, take her case straight to God, and be her most vulnerable self before Him. What great gift, miraculous answer, or deep wisdom awaits us when we are willing to do the same?

$\mathcal{M}$IRIAM

(Exodus 2:1–10, 15:20–21; Numbers 12:1–16, 20:1)

At first glance, the connection points between Miriam's and Hannah's lives may not seem obvious. Hannah led a private life, one of a wife and mother. She was content to let her husband and son occupy public positions in prayer and in leadership. Hannah's life was a quiet one out of the spotlight. Miriam's life, many centuries before Hannah's, was anything but. Miriam and her siblings were front and center among the people of Israel. Miriam's brother Moses, despite his humility and initial reluctance to take the job, had been chosen by God to lead his people. Miriam and her other brother, Aaron, supported Moses in his leadership and, as we'll see a bit later, got in serious trouble when they decided to question it.

The Bible doesn't tell us clearly whether Miriam married or had children of her own. Her life was, though, dedicated to her people and their survival, starting with her brother Moses, the very man who would lead his people out of Egypt and away from the crushing bonds of centuries of slavery. This daring woman was called "Miriam the Prophetess" (Exodus 15:20). Very few women in the Bible have the title, because to be a prophet meant not just to speak the word of the Lord, but also to lead the people into hearing and accepting that truth. It was, by definition, a public calling.

We meet Miriam in one of the most well-known Sunday school stories of all time. It is set against the backdrop of ongoing oppression of the Jewish people. The Jews had multiplied to the extent that the king of Egypt began to fear them, so he cooked up a plan:

"Come, we must deal shrewdly with them or they will become even more numerous and, if war breaks out, will join our enemies, fight against us and leave the country." So they put slave masters over them to oppress them with forced labor . . . (Exodus 1:10–11a)

As Scripture tells us, things didn't go according to plan. In fact, "the more they were oppressed, the more they multiplied and spread" (Exodus 1:12), and this worried the Egyptians even more. The Bible says the Egyptians "came to dread the Israelites" (Exodus 1:13), and that dread drove them to abuse the Israelites even more harshly: working them "ruthlessly," making their lives bitter with hard labor (Exodus 1:14). When that didn't work, the king ordered the Hebrew midwives to kill any boys as they were born, but the midwives refused. When they were summoned to explain why there were so many Hebrew baby boys living, the midwives claimed that the Hebrew women simply gave birth too fast, before they could get there! So, Pharaoh got involved, declaring that every Hebrew baby boy born must be thrown into the Nile River to die. Not everyone obeyed this order, either.

As we're told in Exodus, when Moses was born, he was a "fine" child. If we take a peek ahead to Hebrews 11:23, we see this description of what happened:

By faith Moses' parents hid him for three months after he was born, because they saw he was no ordinary child, and they were not afraid of the king's edict.
When Moses' mother, Jochebed, could no longer hide him safely, she took action.
. . . she got a papyrus basket for him and coated it with tar

and pitch. Then she placed the child in it and put it among the reeds along the bank of the Nile. His sister stood at a distance to see what would happen to him. (Exodus 2:3b–4)

I love the irony here. The Nile is the very river where Moses should have been thrown to his death months earlier. And yet his mother later purposely placed him there in order to save his life. Jochebed knew he was no ordinary child, so she wasn't playing by the rules. Like Hannah, she was sending her precious son back to God.

Sent along to monitor the situation, Miriam was likely just a young girl herself. What kind of risk was she facing? Every male Hebrew baby was supposed to be drowning in that river, not floating along in a custom-made raft. What if she were discovered and someone with less-than-sympathetic feelings toward the Israelites connected her to Moses? Miriam must have had courage, even at this young age. In His sovereignty, God had already written the next, unexpected chapter for Moses and Miriam: a rescuer related to the very man who had commanded that babies like Moses had to die:

Then Pharaoh's daughter went down to the Nile to bathe, and her attendants were walking along the riverbank. She saw the basket among the reeds and sent her female slave to get it. She opened it and saw the baby. He was crying, and she felt sorry for him. "This is one of the Hebrew babies," she said. (Exodus 2:5–6)

Pharaoh's own flesh and blood had shown up and quickly surmised what was going on. She immediately recognized that this was one of the infants her own father wanted killed, and it stirred compassion in her. But, wait! It gets even better. Rather than hiding, Miriam boldly stepped into the potentially life-threatening situation:

> Then [Miriam] asked Pharaoh's daughter, "Shall I go and get one of the Hebrew women to nurse the baby for you?" "Yes, go," she answered. So the girl went and got the baby's mother. Pharaoh's daughter said to her, "Take this baby and nurse him for me, and I will pay you." So the woman took the baby and nursed him. (Exodus 2:7-10)

Imagine how brave Miriam was in that moment. Everything about her would have quickly revealed that she was one of the Hebrew slave children herself. But she took a chance that this woman who had shown such compassion for her baby brother would also have mercy on her, and she stepped forward. Miriam's idea—to offer their own mother to nurse her own baby—was a move of inspired genius. How must Jochebed have felt when Miriam ran to tell her the news? *Mom, come with me! You won't believe this!* Against all odds, her little baby boy was safe and alive, and Jochebed once again held him in her arms. When she heard that a princess of Egypt would actually pay her to be a mother to her own precious child, she must have wept such tears of rejoicing and whispered such prayers of gratitude to God. What would ultimately be the miraculous delivery of His people began with the brave actions of a young girl.

Jochebed would have nursed the baby until his weaning, at around three years of age. And then the Scripture says that when "the child grew older, she took him to Pharaoh's daughter and he became her son. She named him Moses" (Exodus 2:10). Three years was a long time to form a bond with a child, just as Hannah did with Samuel. It is likely Moses carried some memories of his Hebrew family with him into Pharaoh's palace. Because of his time with his birth family, he knew who he was, and he came to identify with his people. It's what prompted Moses, years later, to intervene when he saw an Egyptian beating a Hebrew slave:

> Looking this way and that and seeing no one, he killed the Egyptian and hid him in the sand. (Exodus 2:12)

And it wasn't long before Moses knew that what he had done wasn't a secret. Quite the contrary. Pharaoh found out about it and tried to kill him, and this sent the prophet on an entirely new path, literally. Fleeing certain death, along with the comforts of a royal life, Moses landed in Midian. He was no longer among the people of his birth, the Hebrews, or welcome in his adoptive family, the Egyptians. But he settled there in Midian, marrying the local priest's daughter and beginning his own version of exile.

We don't know how many years passed, but during Moses's absence, things continued to get worse for the Hebrew people. They began to cry out to God, and He heard them and took mercy on them. He appeared to Moses in the burning bush and commanded him to go rescue his people. Safe to say, Moses did not immediately get on board:

> But Moses said to God, "Who am I that I should go to Pharaoh and bring the Israelites out of Egypt?" (Exodus 3:11)

It's a common theme throughout Scripture: the God of the universe, who knows exactly how things will play out, gives a directive, and the human vessel panics. They went back and forth until Moses finally accepted his destiny, and God performed miracle after miracle to win the Israelites' release. Yet, as the Egyptians pursued the escaping Israelites, and as they approached the Red Sea, their faith began to crumble. In Moses, who had rejoined his family, including Miriam, we see an amazing about-face from his initial reluctance:

> Moses answered the people, "Do not be afraid. Stand firm and you will see the deliverance the Lord will bring you today. The Egyptians you see today you will never see again. The Lord will fight for you; you need only to be still." (Exodus 14:13–14)

With their own eyes they witnessed the final miracle that freed them from Egypt's brutal grip, crossing the Red Sea on dry land and then watching the sea engulf their enemies.

And here is where we rejoin Miriam, as a grown woman leading the women's song of praise at the Red Sea after the Israelites' miraculous deliverance. She is an acknowledged leader of her people when she leads the rejoicing after the destruction of Pharaoh's pursuing army:

> Then Miriam the prophet, Aaron's sister, took a timbrel in her hand, and all the women followed her, with timbrels and dancing. Miriam sang to them: "Sing to the Lord, for he is highly exalted. Both horse and driver he has hurled into the sea." (Exodus 15:20–21)

There is so much encapsulated in these short, simple verses. The joy leaps off the page. Moses and all the people have just sung a much longer song of rejoicing, but it is Miriam who reaches for a musical instrument to turn all their joy into dance. Just think of the elation they must have felt. For generations, these people were in the grip of brutal slavery, with no real hope in sight. They were oppressed, and even as Moses sought to free them, they lived through great plagues. When they finally reached the Red Sea, it must have seemed that their good fortune had reached a brick wall. And yet, God tore away that final obstacle so they could be free, and He then used it to subdue their enemies. How could they help but sing and dance? Dancing was a big part of Jewish worship in the Temple, and the Psalms record instances of ritual dance. King David himself danced before the Ark of the Lord.

As witnesses to this exuberant celebration by God's people, we have a hard time finding Miriam next in Scripture. After all that they had seen and experienced together, it wasn't smooth sailing for the Hebrews after they crossed the Red Sea. Indeed, the Israelites would spend decades wandering in the desert, most of them increasingly cranky and unbelieving. They grumbled about the food God sent them and started to miss Egypt, of all places, the scene of their enslavement:

> "We remember the fish we ate in Egypt at no cost—also the cucumbers, melons, leeks, onions and garlic." (Numbers 11:5)

It's easy to play armchair quarterback with this one. How could these people not remember what they'd been rescued from and look forward to the incredible land God had promised them? The truth is they were losing hope. At some point, their desperation even began to fray the sibling bonds Moses, Aaron, and Miriam shared. Numbers 12 kicks off with this blunt statement: "Miriam and Aaron began to talk against Moses . . ." (12:1). Yup, they were sick of their brother taking the lead, which was exactly the role God had assigned him. Remember, it wasn't a role Moses took on willingly. Aaron and Miriam's dissenting continues:

> "Has the Lord spoken only through Moses?" they asked. "Hasn't he also spoken through us?" And the Lord heard this. (Now Moses was a very humble man, more humble than anyone else on the face of the earth.) (Numbers 12:2-3)

In my head, I can hear—just like the "Marcia! Marcia! Marcia!" complaint Jan lodges against her sister on *The Brady Bunch*—the two siblings sulking around: "Moses! Moses! Moses!" Instead of being content with what was theirs, they were envious of Moses's gifts and clearly anointed leadership. And in this they were wrong.

God was burning with anger, and He summoned the three siblings to a meeting. I don't know about you, but I would have been terrified. Terrified. Nothing we do can escape God's notice. Once they were gathered, he called Miriam and Aaron even closer and said:

> "When there is a prophet among you, / I, the Lord, reveal myself to them in visions, / I speak to them in dreams. / But this is not true of my servant Moses; / he is faithful in all my house. / With him I speak face to face, / clearly and

not in riddles; / he sees the form of the Lord. / Why then were you not afraid / to speak against my servant Moses?" (Numbers 12:6–9)

Boom. Whatever Miriam and Aaron thought their positions were, God made it crystal clear that Moses was set apart. He and God spoke face-to-face, with no middleman, no dreams or visions—just God and Moses. And God wanted to know, given that Miriam and Aaron were well aware of that relationship, why they dared speak against Moses. Once the cloud of the Lord lifted, "Miriam's skin was leprous—it became as white as snow" (Exodus 12:10).

There's something notable about this incident: only Miriam suffered punishment, which implies that she was the ringleader behind these complaints. God afflicted her with leprosy, and both Moses and Aaron rallied to her defense. Aaron first begged Moses not to hold their sin and foolishness against them. Moses then appealed directly to God on Miriam's behalf. "Please, God, heal her!" he cried out (Numbers 12:13). God did heal her, but only after Moses's plea and a "time-out" period of seven days during which she was banished outside the camp, with plenty of time and space to think about her mistakes. Scripture tells us that "the people did not move on till she was brought back" (Numbers 12:15). The whole camp of Israel hit Pause, waiting for Miriam to return to them.

At no point in the quarrel, punishment, and reconciliation did God treat Miriam as anything other than a prophet who had made a mistake, despite the fact that her sin played out so publicly. Her leadership of the people was not questioned. Miriam was still Miriam, respected by both God and her people. And here, too, Miriam taught her people a lesson: how to be wrong and still be redeemed. She taught them how to take chastening from God when it was called for and how to own a mistake, even when that mistake happened on the public stage. It was a lesson her people would relive, time and again, as they wandered and sinned and had to seek God in repentance and humility.

Scripture tells us little about Miriam's death, other than giving a terse record of it: "In the first month the whole Israelite community arrived at the Desert of Zin, and they stayed at Kadesh. There Miriam died and was buried" (Numbers 20:1). There must have been a great outpouring of public mourning from her people: now, after their years of stumbling around in the desert, one of their cherished prophets was gone. Miriam held an esteemed and respected position among the Hebrews. Decades earlier, she stood watch over her baby brother, then helped him rescue his people as the Lord had scripted, but she would not see the promised land they were being led to.

So, what are the common threads in the lives of Hannah and Miriam? Each of them watched as a treasured, beloved family member was turned over to God for His greater plans and purposes. And both seemed to do it with the assurance that God was in control. Hannah watched young Samuel walk off into the care of Eli, knowing she might see him once a year, at best. Miriam, too, watched as Moses was launched into unknown territory, first into the Nile and then into the palace of Pharaoh, never knowing when she might reunite with her precious brother.

Both women had close relationships with God, trusting, praying, and relying on His promises. Both had front-row seats to incredible miracles. God reached down into each of their lives and did what was impossible with human effort. Hannah witnessed the miracle happen in her own body, and Miriam saw the miracle on the shores of the Red Sea, as her people survived against all hope.

And here is where Miriam and Hannah reach across the centuries and join hands. Both openly expressed praise for and joy in God. Hannah opened her mouth and poured out her song, and Miriam reached for her timbrel and led the women in a dance of victory and thanksgiving. The joy of both women was the true, deep rejoicing that comes from a life lived in close contact with God. Joy is not the same thing as happiness. There was sorrow in Miriam's life, as in Hannah's. Joy exists despite circumstances, as it is deeply rooted in the steadiness of God's faithfulness.

Where has God been reliable in your most challenging struggles? Where has He shown up, even if it wasn't in the way you anticipated or planned? Each of us has a testimony to share, a song of joy or victory to sing. That doesn't mean we have to stand up in front at church and break into interpretative dance, but we should be excited and motivated to share God's goodness, both with people who know Him and with those who do not. Think of the times you've been moved by a speaker willing to reveal their most vulnerable moments, not to garner sympathy, but to give God the glory. My most painful valleys have made me more empathetic, better able to share in others' suffering, and better equipped to give them words of encouragement—so, why wouldn't I? God rarely calls us to be prophets, but He does urge us each to speak out when He reaches into our lives, to tell other people what we have experienced and learned about God, the specific things we have seen and what they have taught us. It's also how we as women can build a community of support for one another and invite other seeking hearts to join us. In our lives today, may we be as open to sharing our joy as Hannah and Miriam modeled for us centuries ago, all to bring Him glory.

Hannah and Miriam Study Questions

1. The climax of Hannah's story is the Song of Hannah in 1 Samuel 2:1–10. Her song occurs at the end of her story, after she has given birth to Samuel and presented him to serve in the temple with Eli. Why does the Bible place the Song of Hannah here and not at Samuel's birth? Is it important that her song be sung publicly, at the temple in Shiloh? Why or why not?

2. The Song of Mary in the New Testament (Luke 1:46–55) is modeled on the Song of Hannah. Compare the two songs. What does Mary change about Hannah's song? What does she leave the same? How does this reflect the difference in the two women's situations? What does it tell us about Mary that she knew the Song of Hannah so well? What does it tell us about the importance of Hannah's song in Jewish life and practice?

3. Hannah is a wife and mother, and her family is her whole world. It's easy to lose sight of the fact that Miriam is just as much a family woman, even if her family looks a little different. For Miriam, her brothers, Aaron and Moses, are her whole world. One of the clearest places we see this is in their reaction to the leprosy incident (Numbers 12:9–16). What does Moses say when he sees his sister suffering? What does Aaron say? What does this tell us about Miriam's importance to them and her importance to Israel?

4. When Miriam leads the women in rejoicing at the Red Sea, the Bible tells us that "all the women followed her, with timbrels and dancing" (Exodus 15:20). Miriam is the first woman to model celebration with dance and song in the Bible. Take a look at some other examples: Judges 11:32–34 (Jephthah's daughter); 1 Samuel 18:6–7 (women celebrating David); and 1 Samuel 1:20 (women celebrating Saul and Jonathan).

What are the women celebrating in these examples? How was their celebration different from Miriam's? How was it the same? How might Miriam have served as a model for these later women?

ESTHER AND RAHAB

Unexpected Heroes of Faith

ESTHER
(Book of Esther)

Esther is one of only two women in the Bible with a book named after her, and what a book it is! Because of its length, we hear more of her story than that of any other woman in the Bible, and it's got some incredible plot twists, events that required her to muster every bit of courage she had.

Of all the women we meet in this study, Esther is maybe the most unusual. She was the only one who was a queen, for one thing. Hers is also the only story that takes place entirely outside the land of Israel. While Ruth's journey began in Moab, her passage to Israel (both literally and spiritually) was at the heart of her story. But Esther lived only in Persia, along with her entire community, the rest of the Jews who had been captive and who remained there. So, in reading her story, we get a sense of entering a world apart, and that sense of distance—from Israel, from her Jewish community, and even at times, it seemed, from God—is a big part of how Esther's adventure unfolds.

Our first clue about Esther comes in her name, which wasn't

even Jewish. Some scholars believe it's a variation on "Ishtar," the name of the Babylonian fertility goddess and a popular female name in Babylon and Persia, or simply that it means "star." Either way, "Esther" wasn't a Jewish name, but Esther did have one of those as well: "Hadassah," meaning "myrtle tree." In her everyday life, her pagan name would have been the one she used, and this reveals to us a Jewish community that has been uprooted not just from the land of Israel in its exile, but also from their own concept of themselves as God's chosen people. Many years before, a remnant of them had returned from exile to Israel (led by Ezra and Nehemiah), but Esther's family was among the Jews who stayed behind and assimilated into Persian culture. After seventy years in Babylon (then under the rule of Persia), they established homes and families, becoming comfortable and complacent, with a different way of life. Jews like Esther would probably have known nothing of life back in Judea. A young woman, she has already been visited by tragedy by the time we meet her: the Bible tells us she was taken in and raised by her cousin Mordecai after the deaths of her parents.

Esther's is also the only story that takes place entirely in a city, and not just any city, but Susa, the great Persian capital. Next to Susa, Jerusalem looked like a peasant backwater. A huge city of as many as a million people, Susa boasted stunning architecture; its ruins survive today. Indeed, it was the center of all art, industry, and scholarship in the vast Persian Empire. There was nothing in Israel like this magnificent royal city. And Esther likely grew up there, as did thousands of other Jews, because generations before, her ancestors had been captured by Nebuchadnezzar's forces and taken to Babylon. When Babylon fell to the

Persians, captive communities moved into Persian lands as well. This migration of Jews from Israel to Babylon and then to Persia and beyond is known as "the Diaspora," the great scattering of Jewish people throughout the ancient Near East and beyond. This was Esther's world, a sphere where no one she knew had likely ever been to Israel or spoke Hebrew fluently. It's possible that Esther herself didn't know any Hebrew. The Jewish community retained a distinct identity, but it may have been primarily an ethnic one.

We also don't know the state of Esther's religious education. We do know that not once does she utter God's name in her story. It would be understandable if the God of her family and relatives seemed far off to her. Did she know any of the great stories of the women of her people—of Miriam and Hannah, of Deborah and Jael? It's possible she heard about them from her older cousin Mordecai, who took her in as an orphan. Was he also the one who made sure she had a Jewish name and knew something about her roots?

If we live our faith with integrity, we can all feel like Esther at times in our walk with God. As Christians, we're called to live as people set apart from the values around us, often making choices different from the ones our neighbors make. Do you ever feel the same hesitation about those choices that Esther did, thinking twice about revealing who you really are? That sense of "otherness" from the world around us is a positive sign, spiritually speaking. Jesus reminds us that His kingdom is not of this world, and because of that, there is no country, no club, no political party where Christians are fully at home. Scripture tells us that we are "strangers and exiles on the earth" (Hebrews 11:13). So, in a way, the reality of the Diaspora and exile that Esther lived is the one we're called to live as Christians every day—and that's a good thing.

The story of Esther has all the makings of a Hollywood blockbuster. The emperor of Persia, King Xerxes, gave a great feast and summoned his wife, Queen Vashti, to appear before all his nobles, wishing to display her beauty. He wanted to show her off, so when she refused to come, the king's rage was ignited, and he divorced her on the spot. From the very beginning of the story, the king's absolute authority is clear. If he summoned you and you refused to appear, or if you showed up uninvited, you were in big trouble. Both actions were considered exceedingly disrespectful to a monarch, and insulting the king meant banishment or death.

In order to choose a new queen, the king decided to hold a kind of beauty contest and select a new mate from among the most desirable young women in the land. Drafted into this pageant—this would not have been the sort of invitation you refused—Esther quickly became the favorite. Mordecai had specifically instructed her not to reveal her nationality or family background. So, this beautiful Jewish woman became the queen of Persia, living in a palace surrounded by strangers and cut off from her only family.

That's the short and sweet Sunday school version, but this book of the Bible gives us a much more detailed picture about how Esther went from orphan to queen:

Before a young woman's turn came to go in to King Xerxes, she had to complete twelve months of beauty treatments prescribed for the women, six months with oil of myrrh and six with perfumes and cosmetics. And . . . she would go to the king . . . In the evening she would go there and in the morning return to another part of the harem to the care of Shaashgaz, the king's eunuch who was in charge of the concubines. She would not return to the king unless he was pleased with her and summoned her by name. (Esther 2:12-14)

This was the arrangement, and we never really learn how Esther felt about it. From Xerxes's point of view, the whole process had no downside. If he found a woman suitable to be queen, great. If he didn't, well, then he had a stable of concubines. He could flip through and choose a different one every night, the way you or I might choose a movie to watch. He held the power.

But God had miraculous plans for Esther. There was something about her that was different, and Xerxes chose her as his queen:

Now the king was attracted to Esther more than to any of the other women, and she won his favor and approval more than any of the other virgins. So he set a royal crown on her head and made her queen instead of Vashti. And the king gave a great banquet, Esther's banquet, for all his nobles and officials. He proclaimed a holiday throughout the provinces and distributed gifts with royal liberality. (Esther 2:17-18)

This is exactly where a good novel should end: the beautiful young heroine has achieved the pinnacle of earthly glory and has triumphed. But that is not the end of Esther's story—instead, it's just the beginning. Because this is a story about heavenly glory, not earthly glory. It's a story about God's love for His people and about the courage this young woman found the moment it was most needed. The big royal wedding? That's just a blip, setting the stage for the real drama yet to come.

And lurking behind all that is the darker story of the struggle between Haman, the king's vizier, and Esther's cousin Mordecai. Safe to say, Haman had a healthy ego, and he was furious that Mordecai refused to recognize his exalted position and wouldn't bow to him.

> Then the royal officials at the king's gate asked Mordecai, "Why do you disobey the king's command?" Day after day they spoke to him but he refused to comply. Therefore they told Haman about it to see whether Mordecai's behavior would be tolerated, for he had told them he was a Jew. When Haman saw that Mordecai would not kneel down or pay him honor, he was enraged. Yet having learned who Mordecai's people were, he scorned the idea of killing only Mordecai. Instead Haman looked for a way to destroy all Mordecai's people, the Jews, throughout the whole kingdom of Xerxes. (Esther 3:3–6)

Mordecai was not intimidated, and he was certainly not impressed by Haman. To be clear, "bowing" in the Persian context didn't mean a slight tip of the head or a gentle curtsey. No. Among Persians, a bow meant your forehead was on the ground. It meant full prostration. It was a gesture also familiar to ancient Jews, but with one difference: that kind of bow was reserved for God alone. Only in the Temple and only to God would a Jew make such a gesture of ultimate submission. Haman hated Mordecai because the Jewish man wouldn't show him that kind of deference. So, the plot that Haman hatched, to exterminate every Jew in the empire, had at its root Haman's hatred for Jews and the God they worshipped.

Once Haman's plot begins to unfold, Esther's story kicks into overdrive. Haman had cleverly gone to King Xerxes under the guise of rooting out a threat within the region, thereby securing the king's irrevocable backing to unleash a massacre.

> Then Haman said to King Xerxes, "There is a certain people dispersed among the peoples in all the provinces of your kingdom who keep themselves separate. Their customs are different from those of all other people, and they do not obey the king's laws; it is not in the king's best interest to tolerate them. If it pleases the king, let a decree be issued to destroy them." (Esther 3:8-9a)

The king handed over his signet ring and told Haman to carry out the plan, and once it was set in motion, it couldn't be undone. Decrees were translated into multiple languages and spread across the land.

> Dispatches were sent by couriers to all the king's provinces with the order to destroy, kill and annihilate all the Jews—young and old, women and children—on a single day . . . (Esther 3:13a)

When Mordecai heard what amounted to a death sentence for his people, he began grieving, and doing so very publicly. Word got back to the queen, and "she was in great distress" (Esther 4:4). She sent clothes to the man who had taken her into his home as an orphan, but he refused them. She sent one of her royal attendants to find out why he was so troubled, and Mordecai sent back a message with all the chilling details. He also included a desperate request: to "go into the king's presence to beg for mercy and plead with him for her people" (Esther 4:8).

How did she respond in that moment? She didn't say, *Don't worry, I've got it handled.* She answered in a way that reminds us of Moses saying, *Please, send someone else!* As many of us do when confronted with seemingly insurmountable obstacles, she explained why she couldn't possibly be the one to carry out the task. As Mordecai was likely well aware, she couldn't simply show up and ask the king for help—she couldn't appear before him at all, unless he called for her! Anyone who showed up uninvited could be put to death. Mordecai was asking her to be willing to risk her own life in order to save likely thousands of others. His response to her apprehension was both inspirational and blunt:

> "Do not think that because you are in the king's house you alone of all the Jews will escape. For if you remain silent at this time, relief and deliverance for the Jews will arise from another place, but you and your father's family will perish. And who knows but that you have come to your royal position for such a time as this?" (Esther 4:12–14)

Mordecai's question, which turned Esther's life upside down, is followed by his earth-shaking honesty: *Fine, maybe you didn't choose this path, but what if it weren't the king of Persia who chose you, but God Himself?* It may have taken her a moment to digest this reality. Clearly, God had scripted every moment of her life to lead her to this critical position. Mordecai invited her to see that God was the one who had ordered her steps. Faced with a life-or-death decision that held the very survival of the Jewish people in the balance, Esther boldly stepped out in faith.

She sent instructions to Mordecai to call together all the Jews for three days of fasting on her behalf. She recognized that this task was larger than she alone could accomplish. Instead of thinking like a Persian, she was now thinking (for the first time in the story) like a daughter of Israel. Rather than panicking while contemplating an action that could end in her own death, she started by laying a foundation of faith. Alongside her people, the queen humbled herself in fasting. What a powerful picture. At the moment of greatest need, Esther reached out and pulled the Jewish people together in a cry for God's help.

Again and again in the Bible, we see the effectiveness of collective prayer and the power of the people of Israel when they stood united. When God delivered His law on Mount Sinai, it was to all the people of Israel. In one voice, they answered, "We will do everything the Lord has said; we will obey" (Exodus 24:7). The unity of God's people, then, is a heritage we as Christians enjoy today. At our moments of greatest spiritual crisis, we can reach out to our brothers and sisters, maybe strangers by the world's standards, and find an immediate connection. How many times have you heard of someone in need and prayed for them, knowing you'd probably never meet them on this side of heaven? That's the kind of power Esther was asking her people to rally.

Time and time again, throughout the Bible and in our own lives, we have seen God answer the prayers of His people. We can't always explain it, just like most of us can't explain the physics of gravity. But we don't have to understand physics in order to know gravity's power, and we don't always have to understand the mysteries of this amazing gift God has given us, prayer, to know that it works. Esther asked her fellow Jews to join together in seeking divine wisdom and favor. Relying on Mordecai to rally the people, she uttered her famous words:

> **"When this is done, I will go to the king, even though it is against the law. And if I perish, I perish."** (Esther 4:16b)

With this foundation laid, Esther gathered her courage and went to the king. In God's goodness, we see zero hesitation from Xerxes: he extends his golden scepter to her, and Esther is allowed to approach. The king was gracious to her, clearly eager to hear her request. He promised her anything she wanted, even up to half his entire kingdom!

Here the story takes a somewhat unexpected turn, because Esther didn't immediately fall to her knees and beg for her people's lives. Instead, she invited the king to dine with her, but with a very interesting caveat: Haman was invited as well. The element of surprise would be critical in exposing Haman, so why not give him a front-row seat?

Was she lulling him into a false sense of security, appealing to his pride? If so, she was right on target. At that banquet, Esther again demurred on making her request, but promised to reveal it to the king if he and Haman joined her for another banquet the following day. The Bible tells us that "Haman went out that day happy and in high spirits" (Esther 5:9). But his mood quickly soured when he saw Mordecai, who still refused to bow to him.

By the time he got home, Haman was once again focused on topic number one: himself. We're told he boasted to his friends and family about his wealth, about how the king had honored him, about his elevated position and the exclusive invitations from the queen. Then he capped it all off by saying that he got no pleasure from any of it because Mordecai still refused to grovel to him. What advice did he get in response to his complaints? His friends and family told him to have a gallows built seventy-five feet high and to ask the king to hang Mordecai from it. "Then go with the king to the banquet and enjoy yourself" (Esther 4:14). We're told Haman was "delighted" by the suggestion and had the structure built.

What Haman couldn't know is yet another miraculous moment God scripted into this powerful story. You see, that night, the king couldn't sleep. He asked for a book of records to be brought before him. In the pages, he discovered that Mordecai had once overheard a plot to kill the king and warned the king's officials in advance, likely saving the king's life. When he asked what honor or reward the man had been given, the king was informed that nothing had been done in gratitude to Mordecai. That's just about the time Haman showed up to ask the king to hang the man! Instead, the king asked Haman how he could best honor a man publicly. Certain that the king was referring to him, Haman outlined a scenario involving royal robes and a fancy horse, with a prince parading the man through the city yelling, "This is what is done for the man the king delights to honor!" (Esther 6:9).

And that's exactly what Haman got the king to do . . . for Mordecai. Imagine Haman's fury! He returned home despondent, but it was time to return to the second banquet with the king and queen. It was during this elaborate feast that the king again asked the queen what she desired and again offered up to half his kingdom. The time had come, and she laid it all on the line.

Then Queen Esther answered, "If I have found favor with you, Your Majesty, and if it pleases you, grant me my life—this is my petition. And spare my people—this is my request. For I and my people have been sold to be destroyed, killed and annihilated. If we had merely been sold as male and female slaves, I would have kept quiet, because no such distress would justify disturbing the king."

King Xerxes asked Queen Esther, "Who is he? Where is he—the man who has dared to do such a thing?"

Esther said, "An adversary and enemy! This vile Haman!" (Esther 7:3–6).

It was game over for Haman. He was dragged offstage kicking and screaming and hanged from the gallows he himself had ordered built for Mordecai. To top it off, the king gave Haman's estate to Esther and his priceless, powerful signet ring to Mordecai.

But the Jewish people were not yet safe. The king could not undo his decrees opening the Jews up to slaughter, so he allowed Esther and Mordecai to draft a new directive, this one giving the Jewish people every right to assemble and protect themselves, to go after any enemy who came after them.

Not only would the Jewish people survive, but they were allowed to pillage the belongings of all their would-be persecutors. (It is worth noting that while they were mighty warriors who defeated thousands, the Jewish people, as the Bible repeatedly tells us, did not generally plunder the valuables or property left behind.) There was "light and gladness for the Jews" (Esther 8:16), the Scripture tells us, and even more interestingly, the Scripture also says that many of the Persians who witnessed the wondrous reversal became believers in God and converted to Judaism. Could Queen Esther have imagined that? At best, she hoped to help her people survive, but God meant to take her courage and her resourcefulness and use it for the salvation of many more.

It is truly amazing to watch how God took Esther from orphan to queen, and all for the purpose of saving the Jewish people. She didn't have to strive or scheme. He directed her path, every twist and turn, knowing what would one day be asked of her. Often, we're eager to know the path ahead, how something is going to turn out or be resolved. God knows when we're ready, and in His perfect timing, He turns the pages of our stories. What if Esther had known what she would one day be called upon to do? Would she have tried to avoid that first trip to the palace altogether, feeling weak, ill-equipped, or simply afraid of the enormous challenge ahead?

God gave her the tools to be a queen who served Him, and while His name is never mentioned in the Book of Esther, we see His handiwork all through her miraculous story. We cannot know when He will call us to a task that feels beyond our human limits, but Esther's story is the perfect illustration of how He equips us all along the path that leads us to those moments. Just look at the seeds He planted along the way. Mordecai's decision to step in and raise Esther, his concealment of her heritage as she won the king's favor, his position to overhear the plot against the king and save his life, Haman's crippling arrogance—it was all building to the moment when Esther was perfectly positioned to save her people. Nothing is without purpose in God's hands. Esther's story reminds us that God was always working and guiding His people, a perfect foreshadowing of the salvation that would one day come through His Son.

ℛAHAB

(Joshua 2:1–24, 6:25; Hebrews 11:31; James 2:25)

Esther and Rahab make an unlikely pair; one a queen, the other a prostitute. They lived some seven hundred years apart: Esther during the time of the exile in Babylon and Persia, after Israel had been essentially destroyed; and Rahab at the very beginning of Israel's founding as a nation, when Joshua and his troops were just starting to lay plans for taking Canaan. In fact, Rahab is the reason that Joshua's army was able to make its very first conquest, the city of Jericho, so you could say she played an essential role in Israel's later glory and prosperity. But there was nothing glorious about Rahab's life, and if it was prosperous, it wasn't from money earned through an honest living. So, what on earth could this peasant woman from an ancient Canaanite town, a prostitute as well as a pagan, have had to do with the Jewish queen of Persia? Both women were critical to the survival of God's people, placed divinely into position and called upon to step up in a moment of courage.

Like Esther's, Rahab's name points us to some important truths about her. In Hebrew (and in most of the local Semitic languages), her name is "Rachav," meaning "He enlarges" or "He widens." It was a common image of fruitfulness: God enlarging the womb of a pregnant woman, thickening the ear of grain, making the fruit to swell and burst. In Rahab's case, the name has another meaning: to enlarge a land area. Because of her bravery at a critical moment, that's exactly what she helped Israel to do—and that was just the beginning! Rahab the prostitute is one of the ancestors of Christ Himself. She married Salmon of the tribe of Judah and gave birth to Boaz—the same Boaz who would go on to marry Ruth, the great-grandmother of King David, which puts Rahab directly in the lineage of Jesus Himself.

Just like Esther, Rahab changed the world with one bold, decisive act. We meet her in Joshua 2, after some spies from Israel show up at her front door. After forty long years of wandering in the desert without any permanent home, the people of Israel had finally made their way into Canaan. They had become a nomadic people, but they longed for a home. They had lost Moses, and Joshua was their new leader. He would be tasked with taking a band of dispirited nomads and turning them into an army capable of fighting against the trained legions and fortified cities of Canaan. To the human eye, it probably looked like a hopeless mission. The Israelites couldn't match those ancient, sophisticated, well-supplied cities in weaponry or numbers. But after the death of Moses, Joshua had heard directly from God, a powerful directive full of bold promises:

> . . . you and all these people, get ready to cross the Jordan River into the land I am about to give to them—to the Israelites. I will give you every place where you set your foot, as I promised Moses. Your territory will extend from the desert to Lebanon, and from the great river, the Euphrates—all the Hittite country—to the Mediterranean Sea in the west. No one will be able to stand against you all the days of your life. As I was with Moses, so I will be with you; I will never leave you nor forsake you. Be strong and courageous, because you will lead these people to inherit the land I swore to their ancestors to give them. (Joshua 1:2–6)

This is no ordinary pep talk. In the next three verses, God says again, "Be strong and courageous" two more times, adding, "Do not be afraid; do not be discouraged.... [T]he Lord your God will be with you wherever you go" (Joshua 1:7, 9).

That's where the spies come in. Joshua wanted to get a good look at what they were up against, so he sent spies into the mighty city of Jericho. Some scholars believe Rahab was not just a prostitute, but also an innkeeper. The odds are that she made a little money on the side by doing more for guests than just renting them a room. Whatever her loyalties were before the spies arrived, she was willing to protect these men on a mission:

> The king of Jericho was told, "Look, some of the Israelites have come here tonight to spy out the land." So the king of Jericho sent this message to Rahab: "Bring out the men who came to you and entered your house, because they have come to spy out the whole land." (Joshua 2:2-3)

Local inns were clearinghouses for gossip, and it would have been a good idea for Joshua's spies to head to one first, not just to secure lodging for the night, but also to overhear the local news and find out what was going on in town. Unfortunately, news flowed in both directions. The king of Jericho got word that some strangers were in town, over at Rahab's place, and maybe asking too many questions, so he sent his messengers and demanded Rahab turn over her guests.

Here's where Rahab made the decision that changed the course not only of her own life, but of the entire trajectory of human history. She decided to lie to protect her guests, but it wasn't just any lie—it was a detailed one. She admitted that the men had

stopped in, but told the king's messengers, *You just missed them.*
Rahab really sold it: "Go after them quickly. You may catch up
with them!" (Joshua 2:5). But she had already hidden the spies
on her roof. After sending the king's messengers on a wild goose
chase, she returned to the roof for an illuminating chat.

Before we go there, we have to ask the pressing question: Why
did Rahab go to all this trouble? Why did she make what appeared to be an impulsive choice, to lie to the soldiers of her own
king, putting herself and her entire family at tremendous risk?
If the king's men had discovered that Rahab lied, her life would
almost certainly have been in danger. Whatever due process there
was in an ancient Canaanite city ruled by a despotic king, it's
unlikely a prostitute innkeeper would have benefited. There's
simply no denying that Rahab took an unbelievable chance.

In explaining her decision to save them, Rahab told the men
all she had heard of Israel—and what a picture she painted. Word
of God's favor over Israel had spread far and wide. Through those
powerful accounts, God's miracles were paving the way for His
people:

> "I know that the Lord has given you this land and that a
> great fear of you has fallen on us, so that all who live in
> this country are melting in fear because of you. We have
> heard how the Lord dried up the water of the Red Sea for
> you when you came out of Egypt, and what you did to Si-
> hon and Og, the two kings of the Amorites east of the Jor-
> dan, whom you completely destroyed. When we heard of
> it, our hearts melted in fear and everyone's courage failed
> because of you, for the Lord your God is God in heaven
> above and on the earth below." (Joshua 2:9–11)

Rahab knew the reputation of this people and their God. She recognized that God was not like the pagan gods of her day and community.

So, she struck a deal with Joshua's men: in exchange for the help and shelter she offered, they would spare her life and the lives of her family. Knowing what she knew of their mighty God, there was no way she'd even consider turning the spies over to Jericho's king. Rahab knew their God was real and had the power to save her loved ones.

Like Rahab, we all have to experience a moment when we fully understand the reality of God and His power to redeem us. It's the gift of faith, a gift Rahab was clearly given.

Her profession, her nationality—nothing on the surface would have appeared to put her on the path to becoming a part of the nation of Israel and into the lineage of Jesus himself. Yet God expertly crafted her story, leading Israel's brave spies to her doorstep and giving her courage when she needed it most.

Together, Rahab and the spies hatched a plan. Her inn joined the wall of the city, so helping the spies sneak out was an easy task. She lowered them out her window on a rope and sent them on their way, advising them to hide in the hills until their pursuers gave up. Knowing they would return with others in battle, she agreed to hang a scarlet cord in her window and to gather her family inside. That cord would serve as notice to Israel's troops not to harm a single person inside. When the great attack came, trumpets blasting, the people shouting, and the walls of Jericho crashing down, Joshua honored the word of his men. Because of Rahab's hospitality and faith in a God that, up to this point, was not her own, the city was taken:

> But Joshua spared Rahab the prostitute, with her family
> and all who belonged to her, because she hid the men
> Joshua had sent as spies to Jericho—and she lives among
> the Israelites to this day. (Joshua 6:25)

To dwell in Israel was to become one of Israel's people, and it became Rahab's spiritual address as well as her physical one, her place there cemented through her faith and courage.

Both Esther and Rahab made bold decisions to place themselves at risk for the sake of God's people. For Esther, a thoroughly assimilated young Jewish woman who largely hid who she was, revealing her identity and standing bravely before a king on behalf of God's people could have cost her everything—and yet she found the courage. Rahab did much the same, and for a people who were not yet even her own. At times, both Esther and Rahab may have felt disconnected from the people of Israel, but the women's decision to place their own lives on the line made them key players at critical points in the nation's survival. For Esther, this meant being celebrated as the great queen who redeemed all the Jews from death and destruction. For Rahab, it meant being adopted as one of God's own and becoming part of the bloodline of the royal family, part of the bloodline of Christ Himself.

As one of only three women mentioned in Matthew's genealogy of Christ, Rahab was clearly important to early Christians. In fact, she is mentioned two more times in the New Testament, once in Hebrews and once in James, with each mention commending her faith and bravery:

> In the same way, was not even Rahab the prostitute con-
> sidered righteous for what she did when she gave lodging

to the spies and sent them off in a different direction? As the body without the spirit is dead, so faith without deeds is dead. (James 2:25-26)

This is a powerful passage, following just after the story of Abraham's faith—a faith so strong that he was willing to lay down his own beloved son on an altar. That's some pretty exalted company for a Canaanite prostitute from Jericho! James is reminding believers that faith without action is lifeless. Our faith is the intellectual framework that undergirds our Christianity, but unless we use it to step forward in obedience, it lacks real power to change us or the world around us.

Rahab's faith was just a starting point—as it is for us as Christians today. When presented with the chance to breathe life into our faith, will we respond as she did? Will we, like Rahab, understand that our faith must move beyond intellectual agreement and into action? We will all face those critical decisions. In John 16:33, Jesus himself warned His disciples: "In this world you will have trouble." Yet His very next words were "Take heart!," bookended by His unmovable truth "I have overcome the world." May that assurance be all we need when our Esther or Rahab moment arrives.

Esther and Rahab Study Questions

1. The holiday of Purim (Esther 9:17–19) is still celebrated by Jews today, as a commemoration of Esther's triumph. It is traditionally celebrated as "a day of feasting and joy," as it says in the Bible, with carnivals and costumes and partying. But there are lots of biblical holidays celebrated by the people of Israel—Passover (Leviticus 23:4–8), commemorating the Exodus; the Feast of Weeks (Exodus 34:22), commemorating the wheat harvest and later the giving of the law; the New Year Festival (Numbers 29:1–6), commemorating the beginning of another year. These are all joyful occasions, too, but only Purim is celebrated with "feasting and joy." What sets Purim apart from these other festivals? What about this day is worthy of such special joy from the people of Israel?

2. There are several instances in the Bible where people lie in order to obtain a good outcome. Most often these people are women. Rahab lies to keep the soldiers away from the Hebrew spies (Joshua 2:4–5). The Hebrew midwives in Egypt also lie, in Exodus 1:15–21. Compare these two instances of lying and find ways they are similar and ways they are different.

3. What would have happened if the midwives had told the truth? What would have happened if Rahab had told the truth? What are some other examples of famous lies in the Bible? Lying is often a stratagem used by powerless people or people under threat. Are there any circumstances in which the Bible seems to be saying that lying is an acceptable strategy? Are there any circumstances in our own lives where we have relied on lying as the better option?

MARY AND MARTHA
OF BETHANY

Two Pathways

MARY of Bethany
(Luke 10:38–42; John 11:17–44, 12:1–8)

The stories of Mary and Martha are intertwined, woven together around some of the most instructive and miraculous moments in the Bible. And yet the two sisters couldn't have been more different, united by their faith in Jesus, but divided by the ways they felt best to worship Him. Be honest. Have you read their stories and immediately identified with one or the other? I often have, and sometimes a specific season of life has caused me to favor one approach over the other.

These sisters appear together in the Gospels, hosting Jesus in their home in Bethany and at the tomb of their brother Lazarus. Together they witnessed Jesus's greatest miracle: the raising of their brother from the dead. We don't know how the sisters initially met Jesus, but from the moment we're introduced to them, they appear to be part of the intimate inner circle of His disciples. His attachment to them was deep. In fact, the only time the Bible records Jesus weeping is following the death of Lazarus.

Even in the Garden of Gethsemane, facing the prospect of His own death, Jesus was, we are told, "exceedingly sorrowful" (Matthew 26:38)—but for Lazarus, He wept.

Sometimes it can seem as though the Jesus whom John presents to us in his Gospel is otherworldly—calm and all-knowing, given to long theological discussion. The Jesus we meet in John's account is a different Jesus from the one we're introduced to, say, in Mark, whose focus is the suffering servant. John's focus is on the divine aspect of Jesus's nature, yet it is John who presents us with Jesus's most powerfully human moment: the overpowering grief of the death of a close friend. It gives us a chance to see the complete humanity of Jesus, where He experiences our grief and despair. He has lived our trials and can identify with our deepest pain. Whoever else Mary and Martha were, Jesus cared for them deeply.

We often link Mary and Martha in our discussion of the life of Christian service. We talk about being a "Mary" or a "Martha" as though these were separate paths we must choose. But if we carefully read the Scripture passage that introduces these two women to us, we see that that's not what Jesus said at all in response to their sibling dispute.

> As Jesus and his disciples were on their way, he came to a village where a woman named Martha opened her home to him. She had a sister called Mary, who sat at the Lord's feet listening to what he said. But Martha was distracted by all the preparations that had to be made. She came to him and asked, "Lord, don't you care that my sister has left me to do the work by myself? Tell her to help me!"
>
> "Martha, Martha," the Lord answered, "you are worried

and upset about many things, but few things are needed—
or indeed only one. Mary has chosen what is better, and it
will not be taken away from her." (Luke 10:38–42)

There are certain passages of Scripture that collapse all the
distance between Jesus's time and ours, and this is one of them.
Who among us has not engaged in exactly this dispute over
chores? It's safe to say that everyone who has ever shared household obligations with someone else has thought at some point,
I'm the one doing all the work here. Grumbling over domestic
duties has probably been a part of human history since the first
time someone decided the dirt should be swept out of the cave.
We can all relate to the sisters, and of course (given that we all
like to think we are the ones doing the lion's share of the work),
Martha's grievance feels especially righteous to us. It's easy to
see ourselves as Martha.

Because of that instinctive impulse, it can be easy to overlook
the remarkable thing that was actually happening here. In the
ancient Jewish world, women definitely did *not* sit at the feet of
religious teachers. To us, Mary's studying at Jesus's feet might
seem a natural and even touching picture. But to a first-century
Jew, this would have been a deeply shocking image. Mary was
doing three unconventional things: she was engaging in formal
biblical learning; she was in close and intimate physical prox-
imity to a rabbi; and she was seated in a group of men. All these
were taboo in her culture. By welcoming her to sit there, Jesus
was violating every cultural norm that governed how women
should behave, especially in their relationship to learning and
to men. In the first century, only Jewish boys or young men received a formal education.

But, it appears, Jesus disregarded these traditional rules. In fact, He had probably been ignoring them for some time, because notice that Martha's complaint about Mary is not *Lord, do you not care that my sister is breaking all the rules and behaving inappropriately in front of men?* It seems that everyone, including Martha, knew that Jesus was not going to rebuke a woman for taking her place among His disciples. So, Martha had to complain about the *results* of Mary's choice, not the choice itself.

And what was that choice? The Bible tells us that Mary did two things: she "sat at Jesus's feet" and she "heard His word." Her position at His feet shows humility and her listening illustrates her desire to learn. Before she could hear and accept that word, though, she first placed herself in an attitude of complete submission to Jesus. Mary shows us the evolution of getting to know the heart of Jesus, weighing the words and challenges He offered His listeners and ultimately following Him in trust and obedience. Her decision to follow Him wasn't merely an intellectual one. Mary also followed her heart.

As modern-day Christians, we get to know God's heart by studying Scripture, the equivalent of sitting at Jesus's feet. It's our personal guidebook for learning all we can about His nature, His promises, and His plans. It's the way we grow to fulfill His greatest command:

Love the Lord your God with all your heart and with all your soul and with all your mind. (Matthew 22:37)

Mary's story beautifully illustrates the depth of knowing Jesus, both loving Him with our hearts and intellectually embracing Him with our minds.

Mary's actions in this passage mirror the promise of the people of Israel of long ago. In Exodus 24:7, Moses finally presents the full and complete covenant to the people. With one voice, they reply, "We will do everything the Lord has said; we will obey."

The Israelites said not once, but twice, *Whatever God commands, we're in!* They didn't question or bargain. As with Mary, it is enough to know what God commands, even if we don't yet completely understand it.

We see Mary's capacity for deep emotion in two other incidents in Scripture: at the death of her brother and in the anointing of Jesus's feet. That anointing, in John's Gospel, is the last thing that happens before Jesus enters Jerusalem and begins the fateful week that will end in His death, followed by His glorious Resurrection. During His ministry, word of Jesus spread through the region. He was a public figure, and from the moment He entered Jerusalem on Palm Sunday, everything that happened that week played out on a very public stage: the crowds crying, "Hosanna," the teaching in the Temple, the driving out of the moneychangers, the arrest in the garden. It was a whirlwind of a week, and it ended in the most public expression of violence known in the Roman world: crucifixion. What followed was Jesus's triumph over sin and death, His sealing of salvation for all who would accept it. But before all that, He shared an intensely intimate time with His close friends in Bethany, a last moment of calm before the storm:

> Six days before the Passover, Jesus came to Bethany, where Lazarus lived, whom Jesus had raised from the dead. Here a dinner was given in Jesus' honor. Martha served, while

Lazarus was among those reclining at the table with him. Then Mary took about a pint of pure nard, an expensive perfume; she poured it on Jesus' feet and wiped his feet with her hair. And the house was filled with the fragrance of the perfume. (John 12:1-3)

Once again, we see the same dynamic playing out between the sisters: Martha is the one serving, and Mary is the one engaged in a devotional act. But Mary's actions here are even more shocking than before. She is no longer content to express her love simply by sitting at Jesus's feet; now she is driven to an act of physical affection. The Scripture tells us she took out a very expensive ointment or perfume and poured it on Jesus's feet and then wiped His feet with her hair. This gesture would appear to go far beyond the custom of washing guests' feet after they have traveled along dusty roads in the open-toe sandals worn at the time. No, Mary specifically uncorked a valuable treasure, spending it without question on the man she believed to be "the Messiah, the Son of God" (John 11:27). Then she took things a surprising step further. She revealed her hair, loosening it from the coverings that any respectable woman of the time would have worn. By openly bucking the customs of the day, Mary painted a beautiful picture of being fully vulnerable before Jesus.

Judging from the way their whole village turned out to mourn with them at Lazarus's death, Martha and Mary appeared to be prominent in their community. Even so, their relative wealth was the prosperity of a first-century farming family, a family that did well for itself and could maintain a thriving household. By those standards, a bottle of perfumed oil would likely have been a special gift or treasured possession. What's described here is the sort of luxury item sold in big cities, one that elite Roman women and men would have used for their personal grooming. Did Mary have to travel to Jerusalem to purchase that jar? Was it given to her on a special occasion, or as part of a dowry? Clearly, it was of great worth, as one of Jesus's disciples, Judas Iscariot, makes a very public critique of it. We see this play out in John 12:4-6:

> But one of his disciples, Judas Iscariot, who was later to betray him, objected, "Why wasn't this perfume sold and the money given to the poor? It was worth a year's wages." He did not say this because he cared about the poor but because he was a thief; as keeper of the money bag, he used to help himself to what was put into it.

Mary did not justify herself to Judas, whose comments she surely heard, any more than she justified herself to her sister earlier, when Martha complained about her. In both cases, she relied on Jesus to do her speaking for her, and in both cases, His defense of her was better than any she could have offered for herself. He told Judas to leave her alone because "It was intended that she should save this perfume for the day of my burial. You will always have the poor among you, but you will not always have me" (John 12:7-8). What a remarkable thing to say!

Given her household's close brush with death, maybe it makes sense that Mary would find a way to set aside for future use—for the death of the one she clearly loved so much—something as enormously valuable as this substance. After all, she and her sister had anointed their brother's body for burial before Jesus raised him, so she knew exactly what it meant to prepare a loved one's body for the grave.

Shortly before Lazarus's resurrection, Jesus had made clear that His own death was a very real possibility. When he told the disciples that they would all head back to Judea, they questioned Him, noting that Jesus had almost been stoned there (John 11:8). Scripture makes clear that at least Thomas knew what they were risking. John 11:16 records his words: "Let us also go, that we may die with him." Perhaps Mary, too, had a sense of what was to come.

Mary's unreserved expression of love toward Jesus may not have been logical by the standards of her time, but it serves as a clear example of her unabashedly following Him in a way that others deemed foolish. She was willing to break with tradition to do what was most important: learn from and honor her Savior. Sitting at the master's feet in a group of men? Ignoring a woman's expected duties? Making a spectacle of herself by anointing Jesus's feet and wiping them with her hair, of all things? Mary lived out a key lesson: it's not the world's approval we should be chasing. Jesus will serve as our ultimate reward and refuge when we choose Him instead of what the world tells us we should value most.

Mary's relative silence is key to understanding who she was. In fact, the Bible records only one time when Mary spoke. When Lazarus has died, she says to Jesus, "Lord, if You had been here, my brother would not have died" (John 11:21). She stops short of an acknowledgment of Jesus's awesome power. She knows that He will see her pain. Not only did He see it, but He was moved by her grief and shared in it with tears of His own (John 11:35).

Because Mary was the quiet one, and her sister spoke her mind, we get a window into what Martha thought of her sister, but not into what Mary thought of Martha. In all Mary's interactions, Jesus was her single-minded focus. She must have known how irritated Martha was with her—surely, this was not a new argument! It's possible that from the time she was a child, Mary was the one yearning to study, to learn with the men, while Martha was the older sister having to tug her arm, pull her back, remind her of her chores and her place in the world. But with Jesus as her focus, Mary seemed unconcerned by Martha's frustrations or by the norms of the day.

Even though they were such different people, the two women were united in despair. We can imagine Mary and Martha, sitting in that house of grief and desolation, getting the news that Jesus was on His way to them. Their eyes must have met across that room, and the same look of hope would have been written on both their faces. Maybe they both expressed their frustration: "If only He had come sooner." After Lazarus's death, the house must have seemed impossibly empty to both of them. More on that to come—but let's first revisit Jesus's reply to Martha and our tendency to talk about the "Marys and Marthas" of Christian service.

In thinking about the sisters, Christian interpretation all too often focuses on Martha's complaint rather than Jesus's answer. So, let's look again at what Jesus says to her:

> "Martha, Martha," the Lord answered, "you are worried and upset about many things, but few things are needed—or indeed only one. Mary has chosen what is better, and it will not be taken away from her." (Luke 10:41–42)

Jesus's reply is not to tell Mary to abandon her desire to learn from Him. No, it is a wholehearted endorsement of what Mary has chosen. The Christian life calls us to find a balance between cultivating our relationship with Jesus and also serving Him. The trouble comes when we become overly focused on all the things we can do *for* God, rather than on spending time and being in communion *with* Him. Jesus's reply to Martha could not have been clearer: what she was doing was not more important than what Mary had decided to do. Sometimes we struggle with this equation because, at times, service can feel easier. It's simpler to be *doing* something, especially when we can check a box or see the results of our labor. Then we can point to a concrete thing we have done. *See, Lord, how much I love you?*

But God doesn't ask us to prove our love through works. He knows our hearts, and He doesn't need us to prove anything to Him or to other people. It's important not to let the busyness of even good service squeeze out the primary goal of loving God with all our hearts, souls, and minds. This requires spending time with Him, listening, praying, meditating on His words—not just running through a list of tasks.

There's a story about a priest in the French countryside and an old man from the village who would come sit in the church every day. He sat there for hours on end. He didn't read, pray aloud, sing, or do anything but sit. Finally, the priest couldn't resist and asked the man what he found to do in the church for all those hours. The old man looked at him and smiled. Then he nodded toward the altar. "I look at Him," he said. "He looks at me, and we are happy together." This is the deep happiness of Mary—not a happiness that ignores grief or pretends sorrow doesn't exist, but a happiness that embraces Jesus in the midst of sorrow, that sits patiently at His feet and waits for Him.

$\mathcal{M}$ARTHA of Bethany
(Luke 10:38–42; John 11:17–44)

If Mary was the quiet sister, Martha was definitely the talker. We hear from Martha in two passages of Scripture: in her complaint to Jesus about her sister's failure to help her and in her supplication of Jesus after her brother's death. In both these instances, Martha has plenty to say. But let's first revisit that famous complaint:

> As Jesus and his disciples were on their way, he came to a village where a woman named Martha opened her home to him. She had a sister called Mary, who sat at the Lord's feet listening to what he said. But Martha was distracted by all the preparations that had to be made. She came to him and asked, "Lord, don't you care that my sister has left me to do the work by myself? Tell her to help me!" "Martha, Martha," the Lord answered, "you are worried and upset about many things, but few things are needed— or indeed only one. Mary has chosen what is better, and it will not be taken away from her." (Luke 10:38–42)

In looking at this passage from Mary's perspective, we talked about her actions and Jesus's response. But there are things about Martha's words here that can teach us plenty. Look at what she says to Jesus: "Lord, don't you care?" Can't you hear in her tone not only her irritation at her sister, but also her frustration that Jesus is doing nothing about it? After all, isn't Jesus supposed to care about fairness and justice? Isn't He the one preaching kindness and equity? And doesn't He see how Mary is leaving Martha to do all the heavy lifting? Nestled inside Martha's accusatory complaint of "don't you care" is the assumption that Jesus will side with her. I must confess, I've made these same complaints.

In His wisdom and mercy, Jesus didn't tell her to be quiet or go away. He didn't dismiss her by saying, *Why are you bringing your ridiculous little household disputes to me?* He did not tell her that He was a revered scholar, with important things to do, and that as a woman, she had no right to petition Him anyway. He said none of those things, but instead took what she said seriously. That's not the same, of course, as agreeing with her, but He did acknowledge that it was a conversation worth having. Compare this with how He responds to another sibling controversy, in the Gospel of Luke:

> Someone in the crowd said to him, "Teacher, tell my brother to divide the inheritance with me."
> Jesus replied, "Man, who appointed me a judge or an arbiter between you?" (Luke 12:13–14)

Jesus dismissed out of hand the idea that He should have anything to do with the brothers' argument. But this was exactly the sort of dispute someone expected a religious teacher or leader like Jesus to involve himself in—a serious public matter like inheritance, a business matter between men of the community. So, what about a private dispute between women? Such a thing would have been beneath the notice of most teachers, but not Jesus. To Jesus, Martha's concerns did matter. And even though He ended up disagreeing with her, He still listened.

Jesus responded to her with infinite tenderness. He didn't answer in anger, but with care for her soul and an ear for her frustration. He identified her state—"worried and troubled"—and gently showed her a better path. Take notice of the unique way He begins His response: "Martha, Martha," He says to her, and with those words, she becomes one of only three people in the New Testament whom Jesus addresses in the emphatic, doubled form of her name. He says, "Simon, Simon," when He tells Peter He has prayed for him to be strengthened in his time of trial so that he, Peter, could in turn strengthen the other disciples; and He calls out, "Saul, Saul," to Paul on the road to Damascus, when He confronts the Apostle to the Gentiles and dramatically turns his life around. When one looks at His "Martha, Martha" in this context, His words sound less like those of an exasperated parent and more like a serious call to discipleship. Was He asking Martha to reset her priorities in the same life-changing way He transformed Paul's thinking? Martha's call to discipleship happened in her home. Her "road to Damascus" happened to run straight through her kitchen.

Of the three siblings, Martha, Mary, and Lazarus, it was clearly Martha who was tied up in acts of service. It appears she ran the household and took the lead as a woman of action. For example, when she heard that Jesus had come to join the family in their grief, she got up immediately to go meet Him. Mary waited, but not Martha. She seized the opportunity to speak with Jesus:

> "Lord," Martha said to Jesus, "if you had been here, my brother would not have died. But I know that even now God will give you whatever you ask."
> Jesus said to her, "Your brother will rise again."

Martha answered, "I know he will rise again in the resurrection at the last day."

Jesus said to her, "I am the resurrection and the life. The one who believes in me will live, even though they die; and whoever lives by believing in me will never die. Do you believe this?"

"Yes, Lord," she replied, "I believe that you are the Messiah, the Son of God, who is to come into the world." (John 11:21-27)

This is an unreserved confession of faith. It echoes Simon Peter's confession when he says to Jesus, "You are the Christ, the Son of the living God" (Matthew 16:16). But here, in John's Gospel, those words come out of Martha's mouth, out of the mouth of a woman—a woman who, as far as we know, has lived her whole discipleship in her home in her quiet little village of Bethany; a woman who has not traveled all over Judea and Galilee with Jesus and His disciples and who has not been witness (as Peter has) to the many miracles and healings and remarkable events of Jesus's ministry. Still, she knows enough of Jesus to know the truth.

What's even more interesting is the conversation Martha had with Jesus that led to that sweeping profession. Martha was clearly a woman of intelligence and of sound theological reasoning. She began by acknowledging Jesus's power to heal: "Lord, if You had been here, my brother would not have died." But while Mary had been content to leave it at that, Martha was not. She wasn't satisfied with simply making a statement about the past: Martha pressed forward into the future.

Martha's next words are full of faith and confidence: "But

even now I know that whatever you ask of God, God will give you." *But even now*, Martha says. In her faith and trust, Martha believed it would never be too late for God to act. Her confidence in Jesus was boundless, and she alone seemed to realize—perhaps she alone in all of John's Gospel—that Jesus was not bound by considerations of space and time, but participated fully in the timeless life of God.

How many times have you faced despair, when there seemed no possibility of hope? In the world's eyes, and by its faithless standards, it may have appeared there was nowhere left to turn. That's certainly where Martha found herself. And yet, she expressed no hesitation at all that Jesus could overcome even the death of her beloved brother and one of His dearest friends, Lazarus.

At first blush, it may appear that Jesus was simply consoling her: "Lazarus will rise again" (John 11:23). Martha affirmed that, yes, she knew her brother would rise again in the resurrection on the last day (John 11:24). To us, these may seem like accepted tenets of the Christian faith, but in Martha's time and place, they were not universal. In the Judaism of Martha's day, the idea of a life beyond this one was not accepted by the Sadducees, the religious authorities who controlled the Temple and the priesthood. It was the Pharisees, who were in the minority, who taught a more vibrant practice of Judaism. The Pharisees believed that it wasn't just ritual actions in the Temple that mattered, but what happened in the home and in everyday life, too. They also taught that life did not end in the grave, but would continue when faithful men and women were raised with their bodies at the last day of judgment. At times, Jesus railed against the Pharisees, fighting a twisting perversion of the faith. But faith in the final resurrection was one that He did share with Martha. Yet, that's not what he meant in discussing Lazarus in those moments of grief.

Jesus says to Martha, "I am the resurrection and the life" (John 11:5). Martha understood the resurrection to be an *event* that would happen in the future; Jesus showed her that the resurrection was a *person*. Resurrection was not just something to look forward to, far ahead, at the end of time. Jesus was telling her that it was happening right that moment and that resurrection was participation in His life.

This is something some Christians still struggle with today. It is so easy to think of time as a straight line, moving forward in the only way our limited minds can understand. But in the Gospels, Jesus again and again shows us that eternity does not work that way. To participate in God's plan will take us beyond the human limits of time and space. The resurrection is happening now, and what will happen to our bodies at the last day is an extension of what has already begun in our souls. It's a complex theological idea, one that Jesus begins to hint at in His conversation with Nicodemus in John 3, but He fully fleshes it out only here, in a conversation with His trusted friend.

Jesus says to her, "I am the resurrection and the life. The one who believes in me will live, even though they die; and whoever lives by believing in me will never die" (John 11:25–26a).

He goes on to explain the relationship between death and life, and how the life that comes through Him cannot be quenched by death. This, too, tells us things about His relationship with Martha and about who she was. Think about it: Jesus was about to visit a house of death. He was encountering the grieving sister of a man who had died just a few days before, and He didn't mince words. Jesus confidently proclaimed, "Your brother will rise again" (John 11:23). He'd already told the disciples that the miracle was unfolding specifically so that God would be glorified and also the Son (John 11:4). He must have known that Martha's able mind was wrestling with these issues, so He laid out some deep theological principles and asked her a remarkable question: "Do you believe this?" (John 11:25).

Think of other times Jesus asks such direct questions. He explains the mystery of eternal life to Nicodemus, and to the disciples at other points, but nowhere else in the Bible does He stop and ask, "Do you believe this?" It's almost as though Jesus paused to make sure Martha was with Him and that she understood what He was telling her. Was He waiting for her to make the final connection? Because if Jesus was truly the resurrection and the life, as He tells her, then some even more important things about Him must be true as well. Martha made the connection, giving us one of the most complete and beautiful confessions of faith recorded in the Bible:

> **"I believe that you are the Messiah, the Son of God, who is to come into the world." (John 11:27)**

Like Peter in Matthew's Gospel, Martha puts the pieces of the puzzle together: Jesus is the Christ, the Messiah, the fulfillment of all prophecy in the Old Testament. This is what her own observation, combined with her intellectual understanding, revealed to her. But her faith told her something more: that this promised Messiah was not just a man, but was in some mysterious way participating in the actual life of God Himself. Martha was among the very first to make a full Christian confession of faith.

But she was still, of course, practical Martha. As she went out to meet Jesus as He approached their village, was there a part of her that was once again frustrated, wondering why Mary hadn't joined her? After all, the master had come to see them! Was the more sensitive Mary, surrounded by comforting friends and neighbors, too fragile in her grief to run from her home to join them along the road in those moments? Following their enlightening conversation, Martha returned home and told Mary that Jesus was asking for her. When Jesus saw Mary's grief, along with that of others mourning Lazarus's death, He, too, wept and then went with them to the tomb. Here, Jesus and Martha have their last exchange recorded in the Gospel.

> Jesus, once more deeply moved, came to the tomb. It was a cave with a stone laid across the entrance. "Take away the stone," he said.
> "But, Lord," said Martha, the sister of the dead man, "by this time there is a bad odor, for he has been there four days." (John 11:38–39)

Martha wouldn't be Martha if she weren't worrying about the practical aspects of what was about to be Jesus's death-defying miracle. Or maybe she didn't quite understand what it was that Jesus was doing just yet. Lazarus's body had surely been anointed with scented spices and perfumes and carefully wrapped, but even so, the scents and perfumes would have held back the stench of decaying flesh for only so long. Can we blame Martha for not wanting to encounter her brother's body in that condition? She and her sister would have been the ones who prepared his body for burial, so they had had their chance to say good-bye not just to their brother's soul, but to his body. And now Jesus wanted to expose that decomposing body? The thought was unimaginable.

How many of us can see ourselves in Martha in that moment? She had just made a beautiful confession of faith, expressing all the miraculous truths about Jesus. And yet, here she was, just a few verses later, quietly stalling and saying, *No, you don't understand. This is a bad idea.* She was back to seeing with the eyes of the world instead of with the eyes of faith. There is a perfect picture of our frailty in this. As human beings, Christians are capable of statements of great faith, but when our foundations stand challenged by life's circumstances, we can be Martha at the tomb saying, *Now, hold on just a minute. This isn't the way it works!*

Jesus had one last word of wisdom for Martha and for us: "Then Jesus said, 'Did I not tell you that if you believe, you will see the glory of God?'" (John 11:40). He led her right back to her own statement of belief. Sometimes, God has to gently remind us of His promises, and our reliance on them, before He can show us the truth of His glory working in our lives.

Imagine how Martha felt when she saw her dead brother walking out of his tomb and into Jesus's waiting arms? She and her sister were so different; yet their bond in grief was obvious. Surely, they must have reached for each other in that moment of intense, unbelievable joy. They must have held each other and wept tears of happiness—not just at the return of their beloved brother, but at the manifestation of all that they knew to be true of their beloved teacher.

Martha and Mary likely lived quiet lives. They were women,

and that meant certain things for them in their time and place. They had not followed Jesus in His journeys from Galilee to Judea; they had not been wandering disciples. The lives of women in that era were mostly domestic. So, what does it say that Jesus took their private life and turned it into something else? The raising of Lazarus from the dead was among His most public miracles. The whole village was there to watch, and Jesus knew it. When He prayed to the Father, He said:

> **"Father, I thank you that you have heard me. I knew that you always hear me, but I said this for the benefit of the people standing here, that they may believe that you sent me." (John 11:41a–42)**

Because of this very public act, many of the people who had gathered with the sisters to grieve believed in Jesus, and news of the miracle spread like wildfire beyond Bethany and into Jerusalem itself, igniting interest and making the religious authorities suspicious. To many, raising Lazarus from the dead served as Jesus's public announcement of who He really was. Step by step, He had been drawing Martha and Mary out of their sheltered life and into the wider world.

The Gospels tell us that at His Crucifixion, women stood at the cross as witnesses to Jesus's death. Were Mary and Martha there? We can imagine the scene: Martha with her arm around her weeping sister, staring steadfastly at her teacher's face until the very end. Did she think, *How could the One who gave my brother life be unable to give Himself life?* Or did she remember Jesus's words to her at Lazarus's tomb just one week before: *Did I not say to you that if you would believe you would see the glory of God?* Did she remember how He led her gently back to the fullness of her faith? Because she had stood at Lazarus's tomb and watched him walk out alive, was Martha able to stand at the foot of the cross and believe this was not the end of Jesus? Did she understand that she would see the glory of God? What would it be like for us to see that glory in the midst of our own grief and pain and apparent defeat, remembering the eternal truths Jesus revealed to Martha, promises that reassure us even now of the resurrection still to come?

Mary and Martha of Bethany Study Questions

1. One of the most remarkable things about the Mary and Martha story is Jesus's close friendship with both of them, even though they are such different people. Jesus has a gift for friendships not only with a wide range of people—think of the differences in personality of some of the disciples—but with women in particular. What are some other examples of female friendships Jesus forms in the Gospels?

2. Jesus is unmarried, as are many, if not most, of his close friends, including Mary and Martha. He seems to value the bonds of friendship as much as (or more than) the bonds of marriage. Do we live out that commitment in our own lives, with the time and effort we put into our friendships? Do we number both men and women among our close friends, as Jesus numbered both men and women among his? Often, we put lots of spiritual effort into our marriages and into making sure they are filled with holiness. What can we do in our lives to value and promote our friendships as places of holiness and growth as much as our marriages?

3. The Gospel of John in particular spells out the relationship of Mary and Martha to Jesus's suffering and death in Jerusalem. In John, the raising of Lazarus happens right before Jesus enters Jerusalem, and the resentment of the religious authorities over the raising of Lazarus is explicit (see John 12:9–11). Lazarus's resurrection might even be seen as the "trigger event" that leads to Jesus's betrayal and death, and it is the climactic sign that Jesus performs in this Gospel.

Look at the very first sign Jesus performs in John (2:1–11). How is this sign different from the last one He performs? Women are instrumental in both these signs, encouraging and asking Him to reveal His full power—Mary the mother of Jesus at the miracle at Cana and Mary and Martha of Bethany at the raising of Lazarus. What does this presence tell us about the role of women both in Jesus's life and ministry and in the early Church? What can it tell us about our lives today and our own relationship with Jesus?

MARY, THE MOTHER OF JESUS, AND MARY MAGDALENE

Witnesses to the Gospel

MARY, the Mother of Jesus
(Matthew 1:18–2:23; Luke 1:26–56, 2:1–52, 8:19–21;
John 2:1–12, 19:25–27)

The most famous woman in the Bible may, in some ways, be the woman we know the least about. Who were her parents? How and where was she raised? What was it about her that made God decide that this young woman would be "blessed among women"? We know her story so well that some of its most startling facts may not seem so unusual to us. But take a closer look, with fresh eyes, and just imagine what young Mary must have experienced. The sudden appearance of an angel sent with a message directly from God would surely have been overwhelming. Couple that with the announcement that, although she was a virgin, she was going to give birth to a son—*the* Son. It's truly breathtaking. Mary's first thought was disbelief, and she asked the angel, "How will this be since I am a virgin?" (Luke 1:34). But I wonder what else may have raced through her mind. *No one is going to believe this! How will I explain this to Joseph, to my family?*

In learning about Mary—the Mary of Bethlehem with the shepherds and the wise men and the baby Jesus—one good way to understand her is to look at who she was not only at the beginning, but also at the end of this exhilarating and heartbreaking journey. After Jesus was crucified, was resurrected, and then ascended into heaven from the Mount of Olives, the disciples went back to the city. They entered that upper room where they had gathered before, but this time they weren't huddled in fear. This time, they were armed with an invincible promise of the power of the Holy Spirit.

Those present were Peter, John, James and Andrew; Philip and Thomas, Bartholomew and Matthew; James son of Alphaeus and Simon the Zealot, and Judas son of James. They all joined together constantly in prayer, along with the women and Mary the mother of Jesus, and with his brothers. (Acts 1:13b–14)

Mary's presence there, at the heart of the first church, in that room with His disciples, tells us many important things, including (as we covered in the Mary and Martha chapter) that women continued to be a crucial part of the early Christian community. This might not seem strange to us, but in first-century Judea, the idea of women being part of a rabbi's group of wandering disciples was unthinkable. Already the first Christian community was looking very different from the world surrounding it.

One of Mary's defining qualities, illustrated in this passage in Acts, was her devotion to prayer. From the earliest moments that we meet her, she is consistent and faithful in this discipline.

Where Christians were gathered in watchful prayer, there was Mary praying with them. And of course, in the days after the resurrected Jesus left them, the waiting prayer they were doing in that room—waiting for the gift of the Holy Spirit, waiting for the great sign that Jesus had promised them—was exactly the kind of prayer Mary had been modeling her whole life. Her entire relationship with God had been one of waiting for His promises to be fulfilled, even when they seemed impossible by human standards. Who better than she to model for Jesus's disciples what true, prayerful waiting looked like?

Despite their front-row seat to Jesus's ministry and their deepening understanding of all He tried to teach them, the disciples must have had questions. Even after witnessing so many miracles in the forty days after the Resurrection, even after seeing the Ascension, in some moments the disciples likely wondered why Jesus had to leave. After the cross and His Resurrection, they began to fully understand His power and purpose, but they still had questions about His departure. Why couldn't He just stay forever? Was this it? In the midst of the unknown, Mary was faithfully there.

Her prayer with the disciples in those unsettled days was the result of a lifelong commitment to God's plans, even when they didn't align with her own. As we do, she must have grown in faith over the years, watching her son's ministry and more fully internalizing His purpose—which takes us back to where she started: with great humility and patience. Not long after she had been visited by the angel Gabriel, who came with the message that Mary would bear the Savior of the world, we hear her declaration of the mighty goodness of God.

"My soul glorifies the Lord and my spirit rejoices in God my Savior, for he has been mindful of the humble state of his servant. From now on all generations will call me blessed, for the Mighty One has done great things for me—holy is his name. His mercy extends to those who fear him, from generation to generation. He has performed mighty deeds with his arm; he has scattered those who are proud in their inmost thoughts. He has brought down rulers from their thrones but has lifted up the humble. He has filled the hungry with good things but has sent the rich away empty. He has helped his servant Israel, remembering to be merciful to Abraham and his descendants forever, just as he promised our ancestors." (Luke 1:46–55)

Her focus wasn't on the baby yet to come, but on the assurances she already had about the God who sent her the heavenly assignment. We would all understand if she felt overwhelmed by the magnitude of her task, but here she speaks with confidence in His mercy, remembering both the actions she has seen and the promises yet to be fulfilled.

Mary was an evangelist with a very personal mission. She knew great truths about God, a God who chose a humble girl from a backwater Roman province to bring His Son to redeem humanity. This was God stepping inside the course of human history, joining the story of humanity in order to save it. Jesus's arrival would be revolutionary. Knowing what she did, Mary would never see the world the same way again, and she didn't keep this knowledge to herself: she proclaimed it.

She had to know that the path God had charted for her would change the world, and yet her first testimony about Him and

His plans started on the smallest of stages: her cousin Elizabeth's home. We sometimes think the size of our audience is in direct proportion to the impact we can have, but Mary didn't run to the town square. She started within her own family circle, and that's often our most important congregation, the people we love, those closest to us, because they get an up-close look at our faith and how we choose to live it in the most practical ways. This includes laundry and grocery runs and paying bills and cleaning up after the dog—the real nitty-gritty that tests our patience.

The two women shared a most special bond. Elizabeth's pregnancy was also foretold by an angel. Barren and older in age, Elizabeth would give birth to the man who served as the forerunner to Jesus Himself: John. The angel proclaimed that John would bring many people back to God and that he would "make ready a people prepared for the Lord" (Luke 1:17). Watch the beautiful meeting between the two cousins when they share their divine destinies.

> When Elizabeth heard Mary's greeting, the baby leaped in her womb, and Elizabeth was filled with the Holy Spirit. In a loud voice she exclaimed: "Blessed are you among women, and blessed is the child you will bear! But why am I so favored, that the mother of my Lord should come to me? As soon as the sound of your greeting reached my ears, the baby in my womb leaped for joy. Blessed is she who has believed that the Lord would fulfill his promises to her!" (Luke 1:41–45)

Not only had Mary herself been filled with the Holy Spirit, but her cousin Elizabeth had the same experience. Mary's declaration of God's goodness and power was in response to the things that Elizabeth said. Elizabeth had focused on Mary, proclaiming her blessedness and asking, "Why am I so favored, that the mother of my Lord should come to me?" (Luke 1:43). Mary took that praise of her and gently redirected it to the very source of the miracles they were both experiencing.

In between these two poles of Mary's life—Gabriel's visit and Jesus's Ascension into heaven—we see that even she didn't know how her Son's life would play out. She, too, was caught off guard at times, always confident in who He was, but not always in on the game plan. From the earliest days of His life, Mary and Joseph were often on the run, first from Herod, the king who was determined to snuff out Jesus's young life. This threat sent them to Egypt for escape and, later, led them to Nazareth. But along the way, Mary received holy confirmation of the greater plan. Luke 2 tells us the story of a "righteous and devout" man named Simeon. Mary and Joseph met him in Jerusalem, in the Temple courts, where they had taken Jesus to be consecrated, according to custom. Simeon had been promised he would not die before he saw the Messiah. Watch as he sees Jesus:

> Simeon took Him in his arms and praised God, saying: "Sovereign Lord, as you have promised, / you may now dismiss your servant in peace. / For my eyes have seen your salvation, / which you have prepared in the sight of all nations: / a light for revelation to the Gentiles, / and the glory of your people Israel." (Luke 2:28–32)

From before He was conceived, Joseph and Mary knew their Son was special, but look at what Luke tells us about their reaction to Simeon's emotional statement. "The child's father and mother marveled at what was said about him" (Luke 2:33). Even they, who knew about His divine conception, seemed startled by the reminder of His true identity.

Along with Simeon's joyful outburst came a warning: "a sword will pierce your own soul too" (Luke 2:35). Did Simeon's words plant a seed in Mary's mind, a thought that she carried all the way to the cross? We know she was the kind of woman who "treasured up all these things and pondered them in her heart" (Luke 2:19). We're also told about an elderly widow who had fasted and prayed at the Temple for decades, Anna. She, too, recognized Jesus that day and testified to His destiny.

And yet Joseph and Mary were engaged in the day-to-day duties of raising their family and working. So, while we have clear hindsight about His work and ministry, it appears that they, sometimes, had to be reminded. When Jesus was just twelve years old, they all traveled to Jerusalem for the Passover. But when His parents began their journey home, Jesus stayed behind without mentioning it. They were a full day into their journey before Mary and Joseph realized Jesus was not with their crowd. How panicked they must have been. Luke tells us they returned to Jerusalem and didn't find Him until three days later—sitting in the Temple courts having weighty theological discussions. "Everyone who heard him was amazed at his understanding and his answers" (Luke 2:47). They may have been, but Mary was clearly upset.

His mother said to him, "Son, why have you treated us like this? Your father and I have been anxiously searching for you."

"Why were you searching for me?" he asked. "Didn't you

know I had to be in my Father's house?" But they did not understand what he was saying to them. (Luke 2:48–50)

These two people, His earthly parents, had both been visited by an angel and told exactly who their Son would grow up to be. Yet, we see once again that they weren't yet able to grasp the full import of what that would mean.

This moment, for Mary, may have been the first time she really grappled with the idea that her Son was not simply hers alone. She knew this intellectually, of course—the message of the angel had made it very clear who her Son would be. It's one thing to know something with your mind and another to know it with your heart. Maybe Mary thought that the day when Jesus would belong to the whole world was still decades away; to see it beginning when he was just twelve must have been a shock. Luke goes on to tell us that Jesus was "obedient" to His parents and that Mary "treasured all these things in her heart" as Jesus "grew in wisdom and stature, and in favor with God and man" (Luke 2:51–52).

All those years, Mary was His doting mother, balancing an internal dialogue about the days she enjoyed watching Him grow and the years of uncertainty still to come. Years later, we see that she's instrumental in His first public display of His miraculous power. Mary and Jesus, along with His disciples, were at a wedding in Cana. When the wine ran dry, it was Mary who brought it to Jesus's attention. This suggests she knew what He was capable of, but He at first suggested it was not yet time for His public ministry to begin. Rather than pushing Jesus, Mary simply told the servants, "Do whatever he tells you" (John 2:5). Whatever her hesitations had been up to this point, Mary was now willing to reveal her Son's identity to the world. In His first recorded miracle, Jesus turned water into wine—wine so good it baffled the man overseeing the wedding feast. "You have saved the best until now," he proclaimed (John 2:10).

And so began the ministry that would lead her Son straight to the cross. She must have known by then that more sorrow awaited Him once His journey began in earnest, but she didn't try to shield Him. The fear we saw in Mary when Jesus was young had grown into quiet confidence. She knew that He was capable of more. He took the next step in His ministry that day—and came one step closer to the brutal death that would pave the way for a lost world's salvation.

Mary, His own mother, was there at the foot of the cross as He died. To even try to imagine her grief is too much for most of us to bear. Her precious Son—heralded by angels, celebrated by prophets, and lauded as a brilliant scholar—died a public death, with her as a witness. Was there some part of her that wondered if God's plan had gone terribly wrong? Had she misunderstood the destiny she thought had been mapped out for her Son?

In His great compassion, in the midst of His agony, Jesus looked directly at her:

When Jesus saw his mother there, and the disciple whom he loved standing nearby, he said to her, "Woman, here is your son," and to the disciple, "Here is your mother." From that time on, this disciple took her into his home. (John 19:26–27)

Even at His moment of greatest anguish, Jesus was thinking about His earthly mother, the woman who had found the courage to accept her heavenly assignment only to watch it unfold in what appeared, by all human standards, to be a tragedy.

All too often, Christians fall into the mistake of thinking that our journey will always be filled with delight. Mary knew better. The grief and sorrow and pain we experience in this life are real, and we aren't called to ignore or suppress them. Mary's life, grounded in prayer and patience, showed the early Christians that the only road to lasting joy was often through sorrow and prayerful waiting for God. There was no other road to the Resurrection but through the cross, and Mary's life leads us directly there.

Of all the Resurrection experiences that Scripture records for us, Jesus's meeting with His mother is not one of them. What Mary and Jesus said to each other we cannot know, but it must have been filled with the deep joy that transcends temporary circumstances. We can imagine that Mary—the Mary whose song of praise announced the God who changed everything by sending His Son to walk among us—may have had plenty of poetry to pour out upon seeing Jesus resurrected.

The Bible does not record any words of Mary at the Resurrection or even after the Ascension. But there she remains, at the heart of the early Church, her prayer sustaining the apostles. As we are each equipped differently, so was Mary. Her way was unlike the public preaching of Peter or the bold proclamation of Mary Magdalene. Hers was a quieter way, but a deeply joyful one, informed by both crushing misery and unspeakable bliss. And as with the other women we meet in this book, each is assigned a critical role in the story of salvation. As we now take up the challenge to share the Gospel, may we each, like Mary, use our own gifts to declare His glory.

MARY MAGDALENE
(Matthew 27:55–56; Mark 15:40, 16:9; Luke 8:2–3; John 20:11–18)

One of the challenges we find in the New Testament is this: a lot of beloved characters share the name "Mary." It can be difficult to keep them straight. Most scholars think the list looks something like this:

> *Mary, the mother of Jesus;*
> *Mary Magdalene;*
> *Mary of Bethany, sister of Martha;*
> *Mary, the mother of James and Joseph (Mark 15:40);*
> *Mary, the mother of John Mark (Acts 12:12); and*
> *Mary of Clopas (identified as the sister-in-law of Mary, the mother of Jesus, in John 19:25).*

The name "Miriam," from which the name "Mary" derives, calls to mind the great woman of faith who, with her brother Moses, led the people of Israel out of bondage. Mary was clearly at the top of the baby name list for first-century Judea. It might have something to do with the fact that, at the time, the Roman province of Judea was a completely occupied nation, an unwilling part of the vast Roman Empire. Roman troops were stationed in almost every major city and quite a few towns and villages. The Jewish people resisted when and where they could, and in the decades after Jesus's death and Resurrection, they would lead two major revolts against Roman rule. "Miriam"–"Mariam" in the Aramaic–translated in three primary ways: bitterness, beloved, and *rebellion*. So, it makes sense that in a time when people were yearning for liberation, the name would have been a popular one.

The abundance of Marys around Jesus tells us something about who His disciples were. We may have memorized the names of the twelve disciples in Sunday school, but that's not the end of the list. We know from the Bible that the list of disciples or followers was far longer than that. Jesus Himself sent out seventy disciples to take peace, healing, and the word of God into many towns and villages (Luke 10:1-2). This suggests that there must have been a dense crowd of students and followers around Jesus. We do know that many of these were women—not only the Marys just listed, but others, like Joanna, Susanna, and Salome. Remember, Jesus brought something radical into the world of first-century Judea. From the very beginning, He saw the women who followed Him as beloved children of God who deserved a chance to learn about and follow their Heavenly Father.

In all the Gospels, we learn of the devotion and dedication of the Mary who came from the fishing town of Magdala, "Mary the Magdalene." That she is mentioned in all four suggests she was an important part of Jesus's life and story. Luke tells us that Mary and other women "help[ed] to support them out of their own means" (Luke 8:3). Luke also shares an explosive detail: this was the Mary "out of whom had come seven demons" (Luke 8:2). Jesus makes the point several times in His ministry that the one who has experienced the greatest forgiveness will love the most, and Mary appears to have loved Jesus with passionate devotion. In all four Gospels, she is a witness to His Crucifixion, and in John, she is the first witness to the miracle of His Resurrection.

The Resurrection account in John is the most detailed and

tells us the most about Mary. It reveals the Resurrection to us in stages, as the disciples struggle to understand exactly what's happened. John tells us that early on that first Easter Sunday morning, Mary was among the women who went to the tomb in crippling grief, only to discover that the stone covering the entrance had been rolled away. Stunned, she didn't even stick around to investigate, but immediately ran back to the disciples to let them know about this shocking development, blurting out:

> "They have taken the Lord out of the tomb, and we don't know where they have put him!" (John 20:2)

Peter and another disciple broke into a run straight for the tomb. They did what Mary had not, going inside to discover the unthinkable: that Jesus's body was indeed gone. Yet all the cloths used to wrap His body for burial had been left behind. How odd that must have seemed to them.

The Gospel tells us that at this point "the disciples went back to where they were staying" (John 20:10). They were puzzled and confused, and they didn't stick around. The next verse is heart-rending:

> "Now Mary stood outside the tomb crying." (John 20:11)

Just think of the scene. She had followed and learned from her beloved teacher, only to be forced to watch His barbaric death on the cross. Returning to His tomb in deep grief, she was met with the devastating discovery that His precious body was gone. The shell-shocked disciples left, and we see her sobbing by herself. But she wasn't really alone:

As she wept, she bent over to look into the tomb and saw two angels in white, seated where Jesus' body had been, one at the head and the other at the foot. They asked her, "Woman, why are you crying?" "They have taken my Lord away," she said, "and I don't know where they have put him." (John 20:11–13)

It's easy for us to overlook what these verses tell us about Mary herself. She encountered two angels sitting in the tomb of her beloved master, but she didn't cry out in the fear you might expect at the sight of an angel. Was there something about the presence of these angels that was reassuring? Was she grieving so deeply that she didn't recognize them as the heavenly beings they were? In her time with Jesus, Mary had seen incredible miracles. Could it be that her faith in heavenly reality was so firm that she was genuinely not surprised to see angels, even, or especially, in this place of grief and sadness?

The angels asked her a question, and she answered. Simply stated: she wanted to know where her Lord's body had been taken. When the Sabbath was over, Mary and the other women "bought spices so that they might go to anoint Jesus' body" (Mark 16:1). Their whole purpose that morning was simply to go where He had been laid so that they could honor Him in death. The task could not have been easy to consider, but what a privilege these women must have counted it. So, it must have felt like yet another demoralizing blow when they discovered that someone had taken His battered body, the only earthly thing Mary may have felt still connected her to Him.

But it was Jesus Himself who would call her back from that place of ultimate despair:

At this, she turned around and saw Jesus standing there, but she did not realize that it was Jesus. He asked her, "Woman, why are you crying? Who is it you are looking for?" Thinking he was the gardener, she said, "Sir, if you have carried him away, tell me where you have put him, and I will get him." Jesus said to her, "Mary." She turned toward him and cried out in Aramaic, "Rabboni!" (which means "Teacher"). (John 20:14–16)

It's impossible to read this passage and not feel some of what Mary must have felt. The depth of her emotion is palpable, illustrating the enormous loss she must have been trying to process. We see Mary's overwhelming grief in her failure even to recognize Jesus. Her eyes must have been clouded from weeping. All she wanted was a chance to reclaim His body.

It took just one word, "Mary," to turn overwhelming grief into immeasurable joy. In the Bible, the use of the name is the single most powerful way to establish connection. "Moses!" God calls from the burning bush in Exodus. "Saul, Saul!" Jesus calls out to Paul on the road to Damascus. When He wanted to establish His covenant, God not only called Abraham by name, but gave him a new name, as He also did Jacob. Imagine hearing the God of the universe call your name. To be known and seen by Him is to be loved unconditionally, and that is what Mary encountered at the tomb.

Instead of calling Him by name, the Bible tells us that Mary called Him "Teacher," but there's even more to it. *Rabboni* means not just "teacher," but "*my* teacher." And in this one word we see the foundations of Mary's relationship to Jesus. She acknowledged Him as a teacher and master, but this doesn't fully describe their bond. To admit that Jesus is *the* teacher is to see only part of the equation. He needs to be *our* teacher, one with whom we actually have a two-way relationship. "Rabboni" was a title of affection, almost the equivalent of "my dear teacher." In response to Jesus's calling her by name, she called Him by the most descriptive title available.

What else did Mary do? The Bible tells us what Jesus said to her:

> "Do not hold on to me, for I have not yet ascended to the Father. Go instead to my brothers and tell them, 'I am ascending to my Father and your Father, to my God and your God.'" (John 20:17)

It appears that Mary's first reaction when she met her risen Lord was to reach for Him, to touch Him—in fact, to *cling* to Him. She didn't stop to ask questions or to wonder how it was that this thing was happening. She didn't do anything but reach for Him to embrace Him, as I imagine most of us would do in such astounding circumstances. For observant Jews, casual contact between men and women, however innocent, was not allowed. It would have been expected for Jesus, as a rabbi, to forbid most women from touching Him, much less embracing Him. In many ways, though, He had disregarded the cultural norms that separated Him from ministering to people in more personal ways. It seems Mary didn't hesitate to reach out to Him, as if she knew it was permissible. Jesus stopped her embrace only because His glorified body was something very different and new.

Jesus also gave Mary a very specific job. He told her to "go to my brothers" (John 20:17), a word He hadn't previously used for His disciples.

> "[T]ell them, 'I am ascending to my Father and your Father, to my God and your God.'" (John 20:17)

In those words, Jesus is describing them all as one family, joint heirs. As much as she may have wanted to stay in His presence, the Bible gives no indication that Mary vacillated in obeying His command:

> Mary Magdalene went to the disciples with the news: "I have seen the Lord!" And she told them that he had said these things to her. (John 20:18)

At this point, we know that the disciples were still gathered together and had not scattered. And we know that they were afraid: "the doors [were] locked for fear of the Jewish leaders" (John 20:19). Jesus's male disciples were huddled behind locked doors, afraid to emerge lest the same mob that demanded the death of their leader also have them killed.

The Bible gives us no indication that Mary was also fearful. She had not been hiding behind locked doors. She, along with other women, had been at the tomb, rendering what service she could to her Lord, without regard for any consequences to herself. Those faithful women then shared the good news of the Resurrection, sent by Jesus Himself.

After Pentecost and the gift of the Holy Spirit, these men went out and preached the Gospel to the whole world. But before they could do that, they had to have the Gospel, anchored by the glorious Resurrection, preached to them. There's an ancient Christian tradition that calls Mary the "apostle to the apostles," because she was the one who brought the news of the Resurrection to them. We see Mary's courage in this passage, but also the men's skepticism:

"But they did not believe the women, because their words seemed to them like nonsense." (Luke 24:11)

What must it have been like for Mary to try to explain to that roomful of incredulous men what she had seen that morning? Did they think she had lost her mind to grief, emotion? Did any of them glance at the others and think, *Sounds like those demons are back*? It takes courage to speak to a room of disbelieving people. But at the heart of Mary's courage were love and unwavering faith—the overwhelming love she felt for her teacher and that she had experienced from Him in turn and her rock-solid assurance that He was who she believed He was all along.

What intersection point is there between the life of this Mary and of that other, even more famous Mary, the mother of Jesus? What can we see when we hold their two lives next to each other? These two Marys inhabited the same time and place, following Jesus in His earthly ministry. They were there at the Crucifixion, but their stories were wildly different before they arrived at the same fateful place. Where Mary of Nazareth inhabited her faith from the time she was a young girl, Mary of Magdala went through a harrowing path to faith by being released from demon possession.

Even though they were such different personalities, Mary of

Nazareth and Mary of Magdala must have spent a great deal of time together—years, perhaps, of traveling with Jesus. Perhaps they were the leaders among the women who followed Him, providing encouragement and modeling a way that women, too, could follow the master.

And after His death, when so many had deserted Him, these two did not. Scores who had followed Him wanted something from Jesus: miracles, healing, even a political revolution. But as the two Marys followed Him, they offered their love and support instead.

What would it mean for us if we lived our lives in this way? What if we spent our lives drinking in Christ's teaching, following His path, living it out in the daily busyness of life? What if we supported His mission and His message in our faithful devotion and focus? It would not be a life of ease and peace. In fact, it might force us to a path of conflict and sorrow, but it's in those most harrowing valleys that our faith comes to life. As the Marys found, at a time when women were not often vaunted members of society, Jesus's unconditional love for them was pure and steady, as it is for us today.

To live as they did (including living those horrible moments at the foot of the cross) would be to live a life of deepest reward. It led them to the indescribable joy of the Resurrection. So, as we navigate this earth-bound life of valleys and mountaintops, we, too, can look forward to the day we hear Jesus say our name with infinite tenderness and compassion. He is calling to us even now, His beloved children, until the glorious day we will see Him face-to-face.

Mary, the Mother of Jesus, and Mary Magdalene Study Questions

---

1. Mary Magdalene is mentioned in all four Gospels, but only in John does she get the starring role in the announcement of Jesus's Resurrection. As we saw in the study questions for Mary and Martha of Bethany, women are important in the first and last signs that Jesus performs in the Gospel of John: the miracle at Cana (John 2:1–11) and the raising of Lazarus (John 11). In Jesus's own Resurrection, a woman's voice and presence are again centered.

   Read carefully the verses in which Mary interacts with the risen Jesus, in John 20:11–18. Jesus speaks to her three times. What are the three things He says to her? How does she answer Him? Why do you think Jesus asks her not to touch Him?

2. Motherhood is a central theme the Bible returns to again and again. We have seen motherhood play an important part in the stories of Sarah, Hagar, Rachel, Leah, Hannah, and even Ruth. Motherhood in the Bible is a way of looking forward to the next generation and to the future of Israel. How does Mary the mother of Jesus fulfill that idea of motherhood? How does she change it?

3. Read over the events of the Annunciation, Luke 1:26–38. What does Mary call herself here, and why? By calling herself "the Lord's servant," to which biblical mother whom we've studied could she be referring? What could be the meaning of that?

4. Mary and her cousin Zechariah both utter songs of praise about the miracle of the children born to them—Mary in Luke 1:46–55 and Zechariah in Luke 1:67–79. Read both carefully and note the ways in which they are different and the ways in which they are the same. Is it significant that Mary sings her song of praise before the birth of her child and that Zechariah sings his after the birth of his child?

5. Mary's song looks back to the great salvation events of the past. What are some events in the Bible that Mary may have in mind when she says, "He has performed mighty deeds with his arm" (Luke 1:51)? What might she have in mind when she says that He "has lifted up the humble" (Luke 1:52)?

In this book we have looked at pairs of women in the hope that when we hold one life next to the other, we can see things we might not have seen otherwise—ways the women are alike, ways they are different, ways in which one woman's life might speak to another's. We have considered different ideas and interpretations. But as Christians, we are always reading Scripture in light of the Gospel, meaning Christ and His message of salvation is the center of it all. Looking at the Bible through the lens of our own thoughts and ideas is like shining a flashlight on just one side of an object. Sure, it can tell us a lot of important things, but looking at it through Christ is like turning on all the lights in the room. We can see everything all at once, instead of in bits and pieces.

All this is to say, Jesus is the end point of all our searching, so it's fitting that He is the finale of this book. The life of every woman we have looked at can be best understood in Christ. Some of the women we have studied were fortunate enough to know Jesus in person and to be with Him as He walked among us here on earth. Some of them lived long, long before His time, yet we can see the miraculous way they were woven into His story long before Jesus arrived in human form. Still, there are other women we haven't yet met in the pages of this book: women who lived in the time of Christ, who knew Him or interacted with Him, but whose names we don't know. All we know about each of them is found in a few passages in the Gospels, but their stories are incredibly rich. There is so much we can draw from them for application to our lives today.

Again and again, we see Jesus interacting with women who needed compassion, whether because of their own actions or because of circumstances beyond their control. He didn't shy away from sinners or women with no status. In fact, He walked right into their stories and into their lives in a way that not only offered them hope centuries ago, but also provide encouragement and inspiration for us today.

⦵WOMEN

Accused

One of the most striking examples comes in the story of a woman accused of adultery who has been dragged before Jesus as He is teaching in the Temple courts. We're told that people had gathered all around Him to listen to His words, so this woman was being outed in front of a crowd. In those days, an accusation of adultery required witnesses, so I've often wondered how these experts in the law and religious leaders (Pharisees) happened upon her. And what about the man she was with? We don't get those answers, only this challenge from the accusers:

> [They] said to Jesus, "Teacher, this woman was caught in the act of adultery. In the Law Moses commanded us to stone such women. Now what do you say?" They were using this question as a trap, in order to have a basis for accusing him. (John 8:5-6)

These so-called authorities knew much more than they were saying. There is zero doubt they would have known that the law called for *both* the man and woman accused of adultery to be put to death (Leviticus 20:10; Deuteronomy 22:22). Why, if they were so confident in their interpretations, were they always trying to trip up Jesus?

Rather than take the bait, Jesus began writing on the ground with His finger, we're told. We don't know what the words or images were, but we know the Pharisees' questioning continued.

When Jesus finally stood up to speak, I imagine a hush falling over the crowd, now on the edge of their seats over this unexpected twist. He said:

> "Let any one of you who is without sin be the first to throw a stone at her." (John 8:7b)

Ouch! He didn't say, *You're right. The law says we should kill her right now.* He could have said that and more. Instead, He turned the crowd's own phony piety against them—and boy, was it effective!

> At this, those who heard began to go away one at a time, the older ones first, until only Jesus was left, with the woman still standing there. (John 8:9)

There was no stampede to get out of there as Jesus returned to whatever He was writing on the ground. Nope. It sure sounds like these learned experts, shamed into silence as His words sank in, slunk away quietly and slowly. They had no response. None of us is blameless, and they knew it.

We next see a breathtakingly beautiful interaction between Jesus and a woman publicly humiliated and facing a death sentence:

> Jesus straightened up and asked her, "Woman, where are they? Has no one condemned you?"
> "No one, sir," she said.
> "Then neither do I condemn you," Jesus declared. "Go now and leave your life of sin." (John 8:10-11)

To be clear, Jesus wasn't approving of her conduct. To condemn her would have been akin to pronouncing a legal verdict or sentence. Jesus indicated that none of the experts in law or religious leaders had stayed to condemn her and that He wouldn't, either. But He admonished her to turn from her sin. He gave her dignity and a second chance, as He does for us every single time we fall.

The woman in John 8 wasn't the only woman in sin Jesus specifically lovingly confronted and redirected into a new life. The longest conversation Jesus has with a woman in the Bible is found in John 4. Most remarkably, she is not even a Jew—she is a Samaritan, an ethnic and religious outsider. Nearly every dictate of that time would have banned Jesus both from being alone with a woman and from speaking to a Samaritan. There were great divides across race and gender that demanded this conversation in John never happen at all. And yet, the Scriptures tell us that Jesus "had to go" through Samaria (John 4:4). The Greek puts it this way: it was "necessary" that He go there. Keep in mind, the Pharisees and others were so opposed to crossing paths with what they viewed as the very much inferior Samaritans that they undertook elaborate, wildly inconvenient routes around Samaria in their travels. Not Jesus!

Not only did He travel directly through Samaria, but John 4 tells us that He actually stopped there:

So he came to a town in Samaria called Sychar, near the plot of ground Jacob had given to his son Joseph. Jacob's well was there, and Jesus, tired as he was from the journey, sat down by the well. It was about noon.
When a Samaritan woman came to draw water, Jesus said

to her, "Will you give me a drink?" (His disciples had gone into the town to buy food.)
The Samaritan woman said to him, "You are a Jew and I am a Samaritan woman. How can you ask me for a drink?" (For Jews do not associate with Samaritans.) (John 4:5-9)

Once again, Jesus was upending the conventional thinking of the time. One of the clearest messages, among many, we can take from this passage is this: there is no room for sexism or racism in the kingdom of God. Christ is about reaching the person right where they were, regardless of societal norms.

Let's also take note of the timing here. This woman was at the well in the heat of the day, not at a time when most women would have traveled there. The more common scene would have been ladies sharing the trip with their heavy pottery or jugs in tow, trading bits of news or gossip, at a cooler point in the day. Not this woman. She went when the conditions were so unpleasant that she wouldn't have had any company. As we'll come to see, she was an outcast, yet another "undesirable," yet she was so precious in Jesus's sight that He intentionally went to her, just as she was.

Jesus was the first to speak, and He asked her to give Him a drink. The woman was shocked. What was a Jewish man (and it was probably evident that he was not just any Jewish man, but a rabbi) doing asking her for a drink? From the Jewish point of view, Samaritans were blasphemers, heretics, little better than idolaters. They kept a form of Judaism, but nothing like the Temple-based religion Jesus knew. None of this mattered to Christ. He had gone to that well to speak to this pariah of a woman:

Jesus answered her, "If you knew the gift of God and who it is that asks you for a drink, you would have asked him and he would have given you living water."

"Sir," the woman said, "you have nothing to draw with and the well is deep. Where can you get this living water? Are you greater than our father Jacob, who gave us the well and drank from it himself, as did also his sons and his livestock?" (John 4:10–12)

It's worth pausing here to note how Jesus spoke to this marginalized woman. It's a method His disciples asked Him about several times. They always wanted to know why it was that He spoke in indirect, roundabout ways—in parables and metaphors. Often with His disciples, it was about spurring them to deeper thinking. They would be sent out to share the truth of Christ with the world, but in order for that to happen, they had to fully and deeply understand the heart of Jesus's message. Needless to say, there was a learning curve; it didn't happen all at once. Here we can see Jesus's wisdom again, as He speaks to the Samaritan woman in a way that is initially confusing, but that leads her to understand the deeper truth.

Jesus was engaging her in conversation, getting to know her and demonstrating concern for who she was. The dialogue He started with her sparked an opportunity for connection and persuasion. He wasn't there to win a debate, but to share a truth. She'd come to understand that He really saw her, an important ingredient for all of us striving to share His message. This led her to pose a very important question about "living water"—one that Jesus was ready to answer:

"Everyone who drinks this water will be thirsty again, but whoever drinks the water I give them will never thirst. Indeed, the water I give them will become in them a spring of water welling up to eternal life." (John 4:13–14)

The woman was fascinated. What on earth could this man be talking about? She might not have understood it, but she knew what it meant to be thirsty. She knew what it meant to have to drag herself down the long, dusty road to the well to get that precious load of water each day. If this strange Jewish rabbi had a magical way to make sure she would never have to do that again, she was all in!

The woman said to him, "Sir, give me this water so that I won't get thirsty and have to keep coming here to draw water." (John 4:15)

Of course, Jesus and the woman were talking apples and oranges. He was talking about a spiritual truth, and she was resolutely stuck on earthly reality. But notice that Jesus didn't try to argue her out of that position. He didn't say, *No, no, don't you understand that I'm talking theology here?* Instead, He guided her to the conclusion that changed her life forever.

Sometimes we experience the same thing when we meet Jesus at the well. For us, that means coming to the pages of Scripture or in humble prayer and sitting with Him there. We don't have to be scholars. We can grow to understand His most complex lessons through studying His word and seeking wisdom in prayer. It's up to us to take the principles we find there and to apply them in our everyday lives. As James writes, "Anyone who listens to the word but does not do what it says is like someone who looks at his face in a mirror and, after looking at himself, goes away and immediately forgets what he looks like" (James 1:23–24).

Jesus made the application of His truth a very personal connection for the Samaritan woman:

> He told her, "Go, call your husband and come back." (John 4:15–16)

Uh-oh. Here's where things got very uncomfortable for the woman. This was probably the reason she was out at the well in the heat of the day, alone:

> "I have no husband," she replied.
> Jesus said to her, "You are right when you say you have no husband. The fact is, you have had five husbands, and the man you now have is not your husband. What you have just said is quite true." (John 4:17–18)

He really *saw* her, He knew. She wasn't ready to acknowledge the depth of His piercing words . . . not yet. Instead, she turned to a theological debate:

> "Sir," the woman said, "I can see that you are a prophet. Our ancestors worshiped on this mountain, but you Jews claim that the place where we must worship is in Jerusalem." (John 4:19–20)

Okay, you may be some kind of special prophet, but you and I don't even agree on the most basic religious tenets, she says. Jesus came to throw all that aside. What He said next was the key to everything He wanted to communicate to this outsider:

> "Woman," Jesus replied, "believe me, a time is coming when you will worship the Father neither on this mountain nor in Jerusalem. You Samaritans worship what you do not know; we worship what we do know, for salvation is from the Jews. Yet a time is coming and has now come when the true worshipers will worship the Father in the Spirit and in truth, for they are the kind of worshipers the Father seeks. God is spirit, and his worshipers must worship in the Spirit and in truth." (John 4:21–24)

Guess what, Jesus tells her, it's not about the ritual or the place. The time is coming when God cares about you following Him in the Spirit and in truth. No one is going to care what mountaintop you're on when you decide to give Him glory!

Okay, she says, *I hear you, but someone is coming who will straighten all this out*:

> The woman said, "I know that Messiah" (called Christ) "is coming. When he comes, he will explain everything to us." Then Jesus declared, "I, the one speaking to you—I am he." (John 4:25–26)

Wait a minute! Jesus decided that this was the time and place when He would proclaim that He was the Messiah, and to this person, a Samaritan woman. He wasn't in the Temple courts teaching. He wasn't standing on a mountaintop as thousands hung on His every word. He was talking to a woman who, by every rule of the day, He shouldn't even have acknowledged. Yet He reached into her world and dropped a truth bomb—and boy, did it have a ripple effect!

First, the return of the disciples. The Scriptures tell us that the disciples were surprised to find Jesus talking with a woman, but not a single one of them asked an awkward question about what He was doing. Had they finally started to internalize the fact that Jesus wasn't bound by human standards and expectations? So much of what He had done in His ministry was revolutionary, and this time they weren't about to question His judgment.

The woman was so stunned that she left her water jug behind and went running: "Come, see a man who told me everything I ever did. Could this be the Messiah?" (John 4:29). This is a woman who had been slinking around in the shadows, trying to avoid the judging eyes of others. She knew they viewed her as a failure, a serial fornicator. But now she'd encountered something, someone, so radical and miraculous that she didn't want to hide anymore. Jesus didn't win her over by scoring points in a heated debate. He connected with her, showed concern for her and helped her discover an amazing, life-changing truth.

What Jesus said to her was incredible, but what was even more stunning was what He didn't say. He didn't tell her, *Before you can become my messenger, you need to go get rid of your sleazy boyfriend.* He didn't insist that she clean up everything in her life before she could possibly accept His message. How many of us do exactly the opposite of what the Samaritan woman did here? If you've ever been fortunate enough to have someone come clean your home, have you ever rushed around tidying up before the cleaner arrived, so they wouldn't know how truly messy your house was? This is exactly what we look like when we assume Jesus wants us to get our lives in order before He can come in and start cleaning up and repairing the flaws and damage we have. That's backward. Jesus enters our lives to save us, and as He does His work in us, our lives begin to look more like His. The Samaritan woman got the order right.

John 4 tells us many were converted because of her testimony, and that testimony most certainly included the unsavory parts:

> Many of the Samaritans from that town believed in him because of the woman's testimony, "He told me everything I ever did." So when the Samaritans came to him, they urged him to stay with them, and he stayed two days. And because of his words many more became believers. (John 4:39–41)

A woman so flawed and shamed that she trudged to the well alone in the most scorching part of the day became the vessel for delivering the good news. The Messiah had come!

What a beautiful picture of grace. Over and over throughout Scripture, we see God the Father first and then God in the form of His Son, Jesus, use people who are not among the top echelons of society as either esteemed religious leaders or aristocratic elites. How much more grace could we extend to one another? What about to new believers who may not know Malachi from Matthew or exactly how to practice Communion? Or those who don't show up in the right outfit or haven't mastered Christian lingo just yet? Rather than silently judge them or snicker at their expense, let's remember each of them is exactly the kind of person Jesus repeatedly used in order to bring His message to life. It's when we are most wretched and lost that we most need

Him. What joy we should have in seeing someone—maybe even ourselves—find His eternal message of hope and truth in the place of deepest sin and need.

These women—one accused of adultery, the other totally outcast and living in a downward spiral of sin—didn't scare Jesus. He met them where they were. And their stories were so important that they are included in the Gospels, not hidden away as some seedy part of His ministry. No! They're highlighted and celebrated, provided as a lesson in humility and salvation for anyone willing to internalize and then live them out. Let's not forget that in John 3:17 we're told, "God did not send his Son into the world to condemn the world, but to save the world through him."

Yes, we've all fallen short. Jesus wasn't about glossing over sin. He came to make us aware of our sin and to pay the price for us. He didn't come to sentence us to death, but to save us from it.

Women

in Need

Jesus also reached out to women who were in dire straits because of where they found themselves in life, battered and bruised by their circumstances. In Luke 7, we see evidence not only of a death-defying miracle, but also of Jesus's deep kindness for a woman in sorrow and distress. He and His disciples went into the town of Nain, and this is the only time we see it mentioned in the Bible:

> As he approached the town gate, a dead person was being carried out—the only son of his mother, and she was a widow. And a large crowd from the town was with her. (Luke 7:12)

This woman was in a devastating position. She had no husband, and had lost her only son—possibly the only person with a real opportunity to provide for her and watch over her. The image we see here is of a woman walking in her own son's funeral procession, crushed with grief and very likely worried about what will happen to her:

> When the Lord saw her, his heart went out to her and he said, "Don't cry." (Luke 7:13)

As with so many other women who may have been viewed as insignificant in their day, God *saw* her. Just like Hagar and Leah, He saw her misery and complete lack of hope. One translation of the story of the Nain widow says that when Jesus saw her, His "heart broke" (Luke 7:13, The Message). He felt the human despair and grief and fear. What He did next sent shockwaves through the region:

> Then he went up and touched the bier they were carrying him on, and the bearers stood still. He said, "Young man, I say to you, get up!" The dead man sat up and began to talk, and Jesus gave him back to his mother. (Luke 7:14-16)

Jesus literally gave the son back to his grieving mother. In this case, she didn't even ask or express faith in Him at all. Christ was simply so moved that He reached out to this woman and turned her nightmare into something beyond her wildest dreams come true. And what He did that day went far beyond just that shattered widow. Luke 7:16 tells us, "They were all filled with awe and praised God." Earlier in the text, we're told that there were large crowds both with Jesus as He approached the town and also with the funeral procession. When they all saw what had happened, they didn't keep it secret. "This news about Jesus spread throughout Judea and the surrounding country" (Luke 7:17). The story of a widow in deep grief provided the platform for a miracle that spread Christ's ministry far and wide.

Jesus often drew attention to women who would have been considered the very least in society as examples to be lauded. Take the story of the widow we see praised in both Mark 12 and Luke 21. Remember, as a widow in those days, she would likely have been struggling financially, probably socially as well, with few resources and little to offer. She would have had no position, no protector or provider. And yet . . . Jesus points us to this un-named woman twice in the Gospels as the role model we should aspire to emulate.

We see that Jesus had been teaching in the Temple courts, a place where religious leaders of the day often posed complex questions in order "to catch him in his words" (Mark 12:13). Just a few verses later, He warns:

> "Watch out for the teachers of the law. They like to walk around in flowing robes and be greeted with respect in the marketplaces, and have the most important seats in the synagogues and the places of honor at banquets. They devour widows' houses and for a show make lengthy prayers. These men will be punished most severely." (Mark 12:38–40)

"They devour widows' houses"—this can also be translated as property or possessions. Jesus was warning that even the very religious leaders who went around with great shows of piety were taking from destitute women at the bottom of the societal ladder. It's in this context that we meet the humble woman Jesus lifts up, a perfect illustration of God looking on the heart and not on appearances:

> There in the Temple courts, Jesus sat and watched.
> Jesus sat down opposite the place where the offerings were put and watched the crowd putting their money into the temple treasury. Many rich people threw in large amounts. But a poor widow came and put in two very small copper coins, worth only a few cents. (Mark 12:41–42)

I imagine a scene in which some upper-crust people proudly paraded in with lavish offerings or donations, happy to make them publicly and with no small amount of fanfare. They knew everyone was watching—and so did this humble widow. She, too, approached the offering box, knowing everyone could see she gave something that was of almost no value by earthly standards. She also chose to do it publicly, expecting zero acclaim and maybe even some scorn. But that's the very opposite of what she got. Both Mark and Luke highlight the widow and what happened next:

Calling his disciples to him, Jesus said, "Truly I tell you, this poor widow has put more into the treasury than all the others." (Mark 12:43)

What? The disciples already knew that Jesus didn't play by the world's rules. After all, they had just watched as haughty religious leaders once again tried to ensnare Him. But even they may have been confused by what Jesus had just said. In the wake of extravagant "large amounts" being deposited, this widow had given a couple of throwaway coins.

But Jesus *saw* her. He knew her situation, and He wanted to make sure His disciples did, too:

"They all gave out of their wealth; but she, out of her poverty, put in everything—all she had to live on." (Mark 12:44)

So much of what the world tells us is important means nothing in the kingdom of God. What did it cost those wealthy donors to give what they gave? The Greek translation here tells us they were giving out of "an abundance" or "what abounded to them." Yet this woman at the end of her rope not only gave sacrificially, but she gave all she had to live on! The woman who was likely invisible to most people in the Temple that day, the person who probably put the smallest donation in the offering, was the star of the show.

She was the one Jesus put in the spotlight not only to teach His disciples that day, but so that her story would ring down through the ages, prompting us to ask ourselves: Am I really giving in a way that costs me something? Am I sacrificing any of my own comfort to further what my church is doing in the community: paying someone's rent, putting food on their table or clothes on their children's backs? This widow, so anonymous that we don't even know her name, is the one Christ chose to show us real giving.

Throughout the New Testament, women are at the center of so many of Jesus's lessons. He was not on any human being's time line or following their rule books about how to get things done. As we've noted, it made Him deeply unpopular with many of the religious leaders of the day. No matter, He was about His father's business—even if that meant healing people on the Sabbath.

Let's take a peek at two women He did this for, in direct conflict with the strict religious dictates of the day. Mark 1 tells us the story of Jesus teaching and casting out a demon in a synagogue on the Sabbath, then traveling on to Peter's house. There, his mother-in-law was in bed with a fever. Jesus didn't hesitate to step in:

So he went to her, took her hand and helped her up. The fever left her and she began to wait on them. (Mark 1:31)

Luke 4 says Christ "rebuked" the fever. Instantly, she was healed and back on her feet.

Jesus uses an even more public healing of a woman on the Sabbath to make His point in Luke 13. There we find the story of a woman who has been crippled for eighteen years. "She was bent over and could not straighten up at all" (Luke 13:11). Once again, we find those precious words, "Jesus saw her" (Luke 13:12a). How many people had probably looked away from this woman over the years, avoiding eye contact and conversation? Remember, many people in that time viewed sickness as a punishment for sin. *What did she do wrong? I don't want any of that rubbing off on me* . . . Yet God looked directly at her and called her to Him:

> **"Woman, you are set free from your infirmity." Then he put his hands on her, and immediately she straightened up and praised God. (Luke 13:12b–13)**

Imagine her sheer joy. Not only had Jesus Himself seen her and called her to Him in front of everyone in the synagogue, but He had set her free!

Guess what: not everyone was thrilled. Luke 13:14 tells us that the leader of the synagogue was "indignant" that Jesus had healed someone on the Sabbath. *How dare He?* He instructed Jesus that people should come during the six days a week set for work, but forget showing up to get healed on the Sabbath.

Jesus wasn't about to let the pious leader get away with this:

> **The Lord answered him, "You hypocrites! Doesn't each of you on the Sabbath untie your ox or donkey from the**

stall and lead it out to give it water? Then should not this woman, a daughter of Abraham, whom Satan has kept bound for eighteen long years, be set free on the Sabbath day from what bound her?" (Luke 13:15–16)

Jesus called them out on their double standard. It was okay for them to water their animals, but not for Christ to set a woman free from years of pain and anguish?

The very next verse tells us that Jesus's "opponents were humiliated, but the people were delighted with all the wonderful things" He was doing (Luke 13:17). Jesus openly challenged the restrictions of the day, and women were often at the center of one of His most critical lessons: you can't choose legalistic rules over people and over real lives that need care and redemption.

All throughout His ministry, and most especially once His miracles became more and more widely known, Jesus was in demand. At the beginning of this book, we met a woman desperately in need: out of options, with an empty bank account and no hope. She had suffered for years from an ailment of bleeding that no one could cure. She had enormous faith, which paid off when she was healed simply by touching Jesus's garment and believing that this would be enough. So, we circle back now to get the rest of the story. That woman had encountered Jesus while He was on His way to the home of a desperate father:

Then a man named Jairus, a synagogue leader, came and fell at Jesus' feet, pleading with him to come to his house because his only daughter, a girl of about twelve, was dying. (Luke 8:41–42)

It's clear Jesus was heading in that direction, but He was delayed by the woman who needed a miracle of healing. Once Christ realized what had happened when the woman touched His cloak, rather than publicly chastising or embarrassing her, He addressed her as "Daughter," praised her faith, and sent her on her way. We don't know how long that interaction lasted, but it was enough to impact the case of Jairus's daughter:

> While Jesus was still speaking, someone came from the house of Jairus, the synagogue leader. "Your daughter is dead," he said. "Don't bother the teacher anymore." Hearing this, Jesus said to Jairus, "Don't be afraid; just believe, and she will be healed." (Luke 8:49–50)

It's hard to imagine how devastated Jairus must have felt at that moment, yet God in His sovereignty knew what was to come. "Don't be afraid," Jesus said, telling the grieving Jairus simply to believe—and based on what he'd likely just witnessed, it's a good bet he was willing to. Disregarding the news of the girl's death, they traveled on to Jairus's home, where apparently quite a scene awaited them. As you'd expect after the death of a young girl, there were people "wailing and mourning" (Luke 8:52). Jesus told them to stop, that the girl was only sleeping. Look what happens next:

> They laughed at him, knowing that she was dead. But he took her by the hand and said, "My child, get up!" Her spirit returned, and at once she stood up. Then Jesus told them to give her something to eat. (Luke 8:53–55)

What must that moment have been like for this girl? To suddenly open her eyes to find herself surrounded by people grieving her death, only to look into the eyes of the man who'd just brought her back to life. She was the living embodiment of a miracle, a story she and her family would carry for life.

This young girl's story is forever woven together with that of the woman who delays Jesus along the way to reach out to Him in both hope and desperation. The two of them represent the most vulnerable members of their society, but Jesus didn't see women as helpless. He looked at the bleeding woman and saw a woman of remarkable faith, courage, and agency. He saw a proud daughter of Israel. And when He raised Jairus's daughter, He said to her, "Talitha, koum!" (Mark 5:41). It's always a beautiful thing when we catch echoes of Jesus's actual voice, using the Aramaic He would have spoken on a daily basis, as with this simple command, translated as, "Get up, little girl!" The bleeding woman and the dead girl were empowered by Christ to stand on their own—and He does the same for us.

Through times of tumult and loss and anxiety and confusion, we know God is with us and for us. In the pages of the Bible, we see over and over again how He shines a spotlight on women who were key players in His unfolding plan. May He give us the warrior's heart of Jael and Deborah, the insight of Sarah and Hagar, the steadfast hope of Rachel and Leah, the devotion of Tamar and Ruth, the quick courage of Esther and Rahab, and the prophetic voice of Miriam and Hannah. And may He give us the love that filled the lives of the women He himself knew and loved in His life on earth: Mary and Martha of Bethany, Mary Magdalene, and His own beloved mother, Mary of Nazareth.

As we see in each of their stories, the women of the Bible are unique. Some of them were brave and believing from the start. Others felt overwhelmed by and unsure of the assignment set before them. Some had great positions of power, while others were outcasts. Some were devout, while others lived in sin and defeat. God even used a prostitute and a killer, and yet she was positioned where God providentially appointed her to be and given what she needed in the moment. It doesn't matter if we view ourselves as weak, inadequate, faithless, or afraid—*especially* if we view ourselves as weak, inadequate, faithless, or afraid—God has us on assignment.

Whether you are currently on a sunny mountaintop or trudging through a harrowing valley, God is weaving your story into His greater plan. Through His word, we are pointed to women who provide us inspiration and encouragement for our own lives today. And anyone who thinks the women of either the Old or New Testament were simply side notes hasn't been paying attention. The woman described in Proverbs 31 is the perfect example. She brings honor to her home, makes business deals, works "vigorously," and looks out for everyone under her care. She speaks with wisdom and doesn't waste her time. With God's help and the examples planted throughout Scripture, we may live out these words:

She is clothed with strength and dignity; she can laugh at the days to come. (Proverbs 31:25)

ACKNOWLEDGMENTS

This project would never have come to life without the tireless efforts of Michael Tammero and Hannah Long. You have guided this precious collection of powerful, challenging, encouraging stories from concept to reality!

Mary Grace DuPree, your endless hours of work and research laid the foundations of this book. The knowledge and expertise you poured into it are evident on every page.

Jennifer Stair and Derrick Jeter, you are gifts I didn't see coming. Your deep wisdom and theological guidance have been valuable beyond earthly measure. These women and their journeys come alive in these pages because of your insights.

To everyone who prayed and encouraged me through the writing process, I owe you my deepest gratitude: Sheldon, Jeff, Lynne, Penny, Will, Debbie, Angie, Joel, Anna, Charlie, Sarah, Martha Ann, Molly, Jo, Christina, Olivia, and, of course—my Momma.

My heartfelt appreciation to Fox News Books for including *The Women of the Bible Speak* in your inaugural class. I've known these stories my whole life, and yet I found fresh inspiration in studying them anew. I pray readers around the globe will also draw strength and courage from these women.

INDEX

ABOUT THE AUTHOR

SHANNON BREAM is the author of *Finding the Bright Side*, the anchor of *Fox News @ Night*, and the Fox News channel's chief legal correspondent. She has covered landmark cases at the Supreme Court and heated political campaigns and policy battles from the White House to Capitol Hill.